speed knitting

speed knitting

BY kris percival

24 QUICK AND EASY PROJECTS

PHOTOGRAPHS *BY* **sheri giblin**

ILLUSTRATIONS *BY* **randy stratton**

CHRONICLE BOOKS

SAN FRANCISCO

Library of Congress Cataloging-in-Publication Data:

Percival, Kris.
Speed knitting : 24 quick and easy projects / by
  Kris Percival.
p. cm.
Includes index.
ISBN-13: 978-0-8118-5245-6
ISBN-10: 0-8118-5245-8
I. Knitting—Patterns. I. Title.
TT820.P385 2006
746.43'2—DC22
2005027444

Printed in China

Designed by **JAY PETER SALVAS**
This book was typeset in Mrs. Eaves 10/12
  and Myriad Pro 9/13
The photographer wishes to thank stylist **LEIGH NOE**, our
team of assistants, and all the lovely models, without whom
this book would not have been possible. Thank you, Atelier
Yarn Shop in San Francisco for props, and to Chronicle
Books — Jay, you're the best!

Distributed in Canada by Raincoast Books
9050 Shaughnessy Street
Vancouver, British Columbia V6P 6E5

10 9 8 7 6 5 4 3 2 1

CHRONICLE BOOKS LLC
85 Second Street
San Francisco, California 94105

www.chroniclebooks.com

For **SIMON** and **HENRY**, so delightful and so very busy.

Thank you to Jodi, Kate, and the rest of the Chronicle crew. Your ideas, imaginations, and incredible design skills are always inspiring.

Contents

introduction

Knitting is a wonderful, relaxing, and gratifying craft. But with today's fast-paced lifestyle, who has countless hours to spend working on a time-consuming, complicated project? Between work, kids, friends, volunteer projects, and the many other tasks that make up a day, sometimes it seems like a struggle to squeeze everything in. This is where *Speed Knitting* steps in. *Speed Knitting* puts at your finger tips twenty-four quick and easy projects that you can whip up in a few hours or over a weekend. Each project is accompanied by a gorgeous color photo; a list of the yarns, tools, and techniques you will need; and step-by-step directions in no-nonsense, plain English. I've left out those confusing abbreviations that have scared off more than one beginner, although a handy knitting abbreviation guide is included *(page 129)* so you can master the shorthand at your convenience. Each pattern also features an improvisation idea that suggests a twist or transformation of the project. Whether you're a beginner or an expert, you're sure to find patterns here to match your skill level. The Classic Skinny Scarf *(page 18)* is the perfect way for a brand-new knit-ter to learn the knitting basics. But if you're a more seasoned beginner, you might want to try the Button-up Pillow Cover *(page 81)* or a Match My Couch Throw *(page 78)*. These projects will help you expand your skills. More advanced knitters will want to check out some new stitches with the Messenger Bag *(page 30)* or Gauntlet Mittens *(page 36)*. The point is there's something here for everyone.

You'll also find loads of lovely gift ideas in these pages. Spend a couple of hours knitting up the Lickety-split Baby Shower Set *(page 84)* for that friend who's expecting or take a weekend to make the Zigzag Baby Blanket *(page 98)*. Furry friends are covered with the Dog Sweater *(page 88)* and Cat Mat *(page 93)*. And of course *Speed Knitting* is full of fun fashions you can make for yourself. Work up a Simple Shrug *(page 49)* to go with that beloved tank top or knit a Fuzzy Capelet *(page 45)* to give the princess touch to your favorite dress.

Speed Knitting is all about instant gratification. With some chunky yarn, big needles, and a few hours, you can whip up a woolly masterpiece. So swing by the yarn store, pick up a few supplies, and get those needles a'clacking!

getting started

Because knitting comes with its own set of tools and terms, it's easy to feel intimidated at first. Before you knit a stitch, consider preliminary matters such as choosing and preparing yarn, the materials you'll need to have on hand, and a few basic concepts behind knitting. In this chapter you'll find a simple guide to familiarize you with the terms and tools you'll need as you embark on your knitting adventures.

yarns

Who knew that there were so many different kinds of yarn? Here are a few things to keep in mind when making your selection.

COLOR

One of the best things about yarn is that it's available in so many colors. Most yarns are dyed in solid colors, but you may also want to look for tweeds, which feature different-colored flecks, and variegated yarns, which contain lengths of different colors. These yarns lend a rich and complex look to a beginner project.

DYE LOTS

You may notice that acrylics and some wool have "no dye lot" written on their labels. This means that the yarn color won't vary from batch to batch. With most wools, however, it's best to buy more yarn than you think you'll need for a project, as dye lots tend to be small and extremely difficult to match. If you run out before finishing a project and go back to the store for more, you may not find a precise match. The most important thing is to choose a yarn you love. Touch it, gaze at it, even smell it—you and your yarn will be spending some quality time together.

FIBER TYPE

I encourage absolute beginners to knit first with acrylic, a synthetic fiber that doesn't fray or separate as easily as wool. Acrylic is cheap and readily available at larger drugstores as well as yarn shops, and it comes in a wide range of colors. Once you become comfortable with the basic operations of the craft, you can move on to knitting with wool and other types of yarns such as cotton, alpaca (*from llamas*), and mohair (*from goats*).

SKEINS AND BALLS

Some yarns come in skeins that you need to wind by hand into a ball. To do this, untwist the skein and ask a friend to hold the open skein snugly over her hands while you wind. You can use the back of a chair or even your feet if you don't have a friend handy. Eventually, you may want to invest in a swift and a ball winder, which are tools that considerably hasten the winding process. Many brands of yarn, and most acrylics, are wound into a pull skein that allows you to begin knitting immediately. When in doubt, ask your friendly yarn purveyor whether you'll need to wind that yarn into a ball.

TEXTURE

For beginners, I recommend traditionally spun yarns without bumps, fuzz, or elastic.

However, as you gain skill and confidence, you're likely to want to experiment with yarns of differing texture and weight. Several specialty yarns are available, including nubbly bouclé, fuzzy mohair, finely spun linen and silk, and plush chenille.

WEIGHT

The weight of the yarn refers to its heaviness and thickness. As a rule, you will use larger needles with heavier, thicker yarn. The heaviest yarn available is *superbulky,* used for thick, textured pieces. A bit lighter is *bulky,* which knits up quickly and warmly. *Worsted* yarn is one step down from bulky. Readily available and very popular, it's the yarn that most patterns call for. The lightest-weight yarns include *sport* and *fingering,* usually used for baby clothes, knitted lace, and finer clothing.

needles

It can be bewildering to walk into a yarn store for the first time and be faced with the many shapes and sizes of needles. Here are a few pointers.

NEEDLE MATERIALS

Metal or bamboo, wood or plastic? I recommend bamboo or wooden needles for beginners, as they aren't as slippery as metal and are warmer to the touch than plastic or metal. You may also find needles made of casein *(a natural dairy product),* designed to feel like antique tortoiseshell needles.

NEEDLE SHAPES

Single-point or *straight* needles are the traditional needles, with a knob on one end, usually used when creating flat pieces or sweater parts. They come in 10-, 12-, or 14-inch lengths. Select the needle length by the size of your project and the materials list given in the pattern.

Double-pointed needles are used for knitting smaller, tubular shapes such as socks and mittens, and for finishing off larger projects knit on circular needles. Double-pointed needles come in sets of 4 or 5 needles to a package.

Circular needles are basically two double-pointed needles joined by a plastic cord and are used for knitting larger projects in the round. Circular needles can be anywhere from 12 to 40 inches in length, allowing you to make seamless hats and bulky sweater bodies. You can also use them to knit flat pieces.

NEEDLE SIZE

Needles come in sizes ranging from 0 *(for very delicate doll clothes and collars)* to size 19 *(for extra-bulky scarves and sweaters that knit up in a flash)*. Most yarn packages specify which size works best for that type of yarn. Knitting patterns will also recommend appropriate needle sizes. If you're not sure of the size you need, ask a knowledgeable person who works at the yarn store.

miscellaneous
paraphernalia

A few additional items will help make your knitting projects go more smoothly. They're inexpensive and will prove useful time and time again.

CROCHET HOOK

At some point you will drop a stitch and not realize it until you've knit a few rows *(or maybe more)*. You can carefully undo your work until you reach the problem spot and reknit, or you can find the top loop of the dropped stitch and reweave it into the fabric with the help of a crochet hook *(see page 113)*.

GAUGE AID

This flat metal tool has holes that tell you the size of a needle so you can quickly find the appropriate ones. It also has a thick, open 90-degree angle with a ruler on each side. Place this directly on your knit swatch to quickly determine the number of stitches per inch.

POINT PROTECTORS

These small rubber caps fit on the tips of your needles to keep your work from slipping off when you put your project down. They fit size 3 to 15 needles.

ROW COUNTER

This is useful when you're first learning to knit. I used mine a lot as a beginner because I was so focused on the basic mechanics of the craft that I often forgot how far along I was and found myself constantly having to painstakingly count rows.

SCISSORS

A plain pair of sharp scissors is an utter necessity when working with yarn.

STITCH HOLDERS

These resemble large safety pins and are used to hold stitches that you've set aside. For example, when making mittens or sweaters, you will have to set aside the thumb-hole stitches and the armhole stitches, respectively, and come back to them later. Some knitters use safety pins, but they tend to snag on the yarn.

STITCH MARKERS

Place one of these small plastic rings in front of the first stitch when knitting in the round, and you'll never have to guess at your starting point. You can also make your own stitch marker with a simple knotted loop of yarn in a contrasting color.

TAPE MEASURE

This comes in handy for measuring the length of scarves and for patterns in which you are directed to knit a certain number of inches rather than a certain number of rows.

YARN NEEDLES

These are a must for finishing any knit project. A yarn needle is a big, blunt sewing needle with a large eye used to weave loose ends into the body of your project.

YARN WEIGHT: CONVERSION CHART

Throughout this book you might notice that yarn weights will be listed in either ounces or grams. While there are no fast and steady rules as to why different yarn manufacturers use different units of measurements for their products, oftentimes light-weight yarns such as mohair tend to

be sold in grams, as it allows the manufacturer to be more precise. This book takes its cues from the labels of the yarn used, and lists them accordingly. It's entirely possible that while shopping for your yarn you might find that the manufacturer has listed its weight in a different unit of measurement than the one specified in this book. In that case, use the conversion chart below.

One important thing to keep in mind is that yarn can be longer or shorter depending on how heavy or dense it is. For instance, a 4 ounce skein of bulky yarn might be 125 yards long while those same 4 ounces of worsted weight yarn might measure out to 190 yards.

It's usually a good idea to pay attention to both the weight and the length of your yarn when estimating how many skeins you will need to finish a project.

OUNCES	GRAMS
1.76 ounces	50 grams
3.52 ounces	100 grams
2 ounces	56.69 grams
4 ounces	133.39 grams

accessories

GAUGE

should be about 1.6 stitches per inch in garter stitch on size 17 needles. Adjust needle size if necessary to obtain correct gauge. Exact gauge is not critical for this project.

YOU WILL NEED

2 skeins (100 grams each) bulky wool

1 pair size 17 needles

Tape measure

Scissors

Yarn needle

TECHNIQUES

Binding off, *page 112*

Casting on, *page 108*

Garter stitch, *page 115*

Weaving in loose ends, *page 113*

FINISHED DIMENSIONS

approximately 5 inches wide by 90 inches long

skinny scarf classic

Here's a basic yet elegant scarf that goes with everything and knits up so very quickly. It's a perfect project to start with if you're a beginner. It's also a terrific project to tote with you on the bus or to work on while you watch TV.

01. Cast on 8 stitches, leaving a 6-inch tail to weave in later.

02. Work in garter stitch *(knit all stitches, every row)* until scarf measures 90 inches long from the cast-on edge.

03. Bind off.

04. Weave in and trim loose ends.

IMPROVISATION IDEA

Mix it up by alternating different types of yarns for an artier, more eclectic look. *(This is also good for using up odd ends!)*

YARN CREDIT

Takhi Yarns "Baby," 100% merino wool, 100-gram ball *(60 yards)*.
Color: #4

should be about 1½ stitches per inch in stitch pattern on size 17 needles. Adjust needle size if necessary to obtain correct gauge.

YOU WILL NEED (SCARF)

2 skeins (2 ounces each) mohair in light green, yarn A

2 skeins (100 grams each) bulky alpaca in dark green, yarn B

2 skeins (100 grams each) bulky alpaca in olive green, yarn C

1 pair size 17 needles

Tape measure

Scissors

Yarn needle

TECHNIQUES (SCARF)

Binding off, *page 112*

Casting on, *page 108*

Double moss stitch

Knitting slip stitch, *page 124*

mossy scarf and hat

For this easy scarf and hat set, you'll need to use three strands of yarn at once. You can either use three strands of the same yarn or you can create your own look with three different types of yarn. I prefer mixing and matching. It's so much fun to come up with unusual texture and color combinations. Tripling up yarns also speeds up the knitting process, so you can make a bigger, thicker scarf and a warm and cozy hat a lot faster than you would using individual strands.

SCARF

01. Holding 1 strand of each yarn *(A, B, and C)* as 1, cast 18 stitches on your size 17 needles, leaving a 6-inch tail to weave in later.

02. Rows 1 and 2: With yarn in back, slip 1 knitwise then work in purl 2, knit 2 across until 1 stitch remains. Knit the remaining stitch.

03. Rows 3 and 4: With yarn in back, slip 1 knitwise, then work in knit 2, purl 2 across until 1 stitch remains. Knit the remaining stitch.

04. Repeat steps 2 and 3 until scarf measures 80 inches from the cast-on edge.

05. Bind off. Weave in loose ends and trim.

Continued

Weaving in loose ends, *page 113*

Working with three strands of yarn at once *(see pattern introduction)*

GAUGE (HAT)

should be about 2 stitches per inch in stitch pattern on a size 15 needle. Adjust needle size if necessary to obtain correct gauge.

YOU WILL NEED (HAT)

1 skein (2 ounces) mohair in light green, yarn A

1 skein (100 grams) bulky alpaca in dark green, yarn B

1 skein (100 grams) bulky alpaca in olive green, yarn C

4 size 13 double-pointed needles

1 size 13 circular needle, 16 inches long

1 size 15 circular needle, 16 inches long

Tape measure

Scissors

Yarn needle

1 stitch marker

HAT

01. Holding 3 strands of yarn together as for scarf, cast 36 stitches on your size 13 circular needle, leaving a 6-inch tail to weave in later. Place marker. Join, being careful not to twist stitches.

02. Work 2 rounds in knit 1, purl 1 ribbing.

03. Change to size 15 circular needle.

04. Work 2 rounds in purl 2, knit 2.

05. Work 2 rounds in knit 2, purl 2.

06. Repeat steps 4 and 5 until hat measures 7½ inches from cast-on edge.

07. Next 2 rounds: Knit 2 together around, switching to the size 13 double-pointed needles when round becomes too tight—18 stitches remain after first round; 9 stitches remain after second round.

08. Cut yarn, leaving an 8-inch tail. Draw tail through remaining stitches; pull tightly to close hole. Fasten off securely on inside of hat.

09. Weave in and trim loose ends.

IMPROVISATION IDEA

For more calmly colored, darker moss, use two skeins of dark green alpaca to one skein of light green mohair.

YARN CREDIT

Victorian Brushed Mohair,
70% mohair, 24% wool, 6% nylon, 2-ounce skein *(145 yards).*
Color: #132.

Reynolds Andean Alpaca Regal,
90% alpaca, 10% wool, 100-gram skein *(110 yards).*
Colors: #8, #15 *(dark green)*

TECHNIQUES (HAT)

Casting on, *page 108*

Decreasing, *page 117*

Double moss stitch

Knitting in the round, *page 119*

Rib stitch, *page 115*

Weaving in loose ends, *page 113*

Working with three strands of yarn at once (*see pattern introduction*)

FINISHED DIMENSIONS

Scarf: approximately 12 inches wide by 80 inches long

Hat: approximately 20 inches in circumference, slightly stretched, by 8 inches high

scenester scarf-hat

This scarf-hat is a two-in-one wonder. Two ends of a long, snuggly soft scarf meet in the center with a hood. With pockets at the ends to keep your hands warm, it's the ultimate on-the-go accessory.

01. Cast on 10 stitches, leaving a 6-inch tail to weave in later.

02. Work 6 inches in reverse stockinette stitch *(purl side is "right side")*. You will flip it up and seam it later to form your pocket. Mark this last row as fold line.

03. Work 6 inches in stockinette stitch. End with a purl row.

04. Slip 1, knit to end of row. Next row, slip 1, purl to end of row.

05. Repeat step 4 until scarf measures 22 inches from fold line. End with a purl row.

06. Knit 2 together, knit until 2 stitches remain on needle, then knit 2 together again—8 stitches total remain.

07. Purl 1 row.

08. Repeat step 4 until scarf measures 28 inches from fold line. End with a purl row.

09. Slide scarf to a stitch holder, leaving yarn attached. Repeat steps 1 through 8 to make the other side of the scarf.

10. Cast on 2 stitches to scarf part 2, then cut yarn. Slide scarf part 1 onto the same needle, keeping the 2 cast-on stitches in the middle—a total of 18 stitches. Knit across to join.

11. Knit 2, place marker, purl 5, place marker, purl 4, place marker, purl 5, place marker, knit 2.

Continued

GAUGE

should be about 1½ stitches per inch in stockinette stitch on a size 15 needle. Adjust needle size if necessary to obtain correct gauge.

YOU WILL NEED

4 skeins (50 grams each) fluffy, bulky yarn

1 size 15 circular needle, 29 inches long (to work flat)

4 stitch markers

Tape measure

Scissors

Yarn needle

1 medium stitch holder

TECHNIQUES

Binding off, *page 112*

Casting on, *page 108*

Decreasing, *page 117*

Increasing, *page 116*

Knitting slip stitch, *page 124*

Making seams, *page 120*

Stockinette stitch, *page 115*

Weaving in loose ends, *page 113*

FINISHED DIMENSIONS

Scarf: approximately 28 inches long and 6½ inches wide

Hood: approximately 16 inches wide; note that the fabric is very flexible

12. Increase row: Knit across row, increasing 1 immediately before second marker and immediately after third marker—20 stitches total.

13. Knit 2, purl until 2 stitches remain, knit 2. Work 2 rows even in pattern, remembering to knit the first and last 2 stitches.

14. Repeat step 12—22 stitches total. Then work 3 rows even in pattern, remembering to knit the first and last 2 stitches.

15. Repeat step 12—24 stitches total. Then work 5 rows even in pattern, remembering to knit the first and last 2 stitches.

16. Decrease row: Knit to 2 stitches before second marker, slip, slip, knit. Knit to third marker, slip marker, knit 2 together. Knit to end of row—22 stitches total remain.

17. Work next row even.

18. Decrease row: Knit to 2 stitches before second marker, slip, slip, knit. Knit to third marker, slip marker, knit 2 together. Knit to end of row—20 stitches total.

19. Work 7 more rows even.

20. Bind off.

21. Seam hood and pockets. Weave in and trim loose ends.

IMPROVISATION IDEA

If you want a flatter, wider scarf, work in garter stitch until step 10. If you want a scarf with a fuller hood, skip the decreases in steps 16 and 18. You can even switch them to increases for a flop-over-the-brow effect.

YARN CREDIT

Karabella Yarns "Brushed Alpaca," 100% alpaca, 50-gram ball *(33 meters)*. **Color:** #1001

belt snaky

Give those old jeans some new life with a long, limber belt. The natural curl of the stitch pattern makes the belt curl into a snake shape all on its own.

01. Cast on 7 stitches, leaving a 6-inch tail to weave in later.

02. Row 1: Purl.

03. Row 2: Knit 1, * yarn forward *(to the purl position)*, slip 1 stitch as if to purl, yarn back *(to the knit position)*, knit 1. Repeat from * to end of row.

04. Row 3: Purl.

05. Row 4: Knit 2, * yarn forward *(to the purl position)*, slip 1 stitch as if to purl, yarn back *(to the knit position)*, knit 1. Repeat from * until 1 stitch remains. Knit the final stitch.

Continued

GAUGE

should be about 3½ stitches per inch in pattern stitch below on size 10 needles. Adjust needle size if necessary to obtain correct gauge.

YOU WILL NEED

1 skein (100 grams) bulky cotton yarn

1 pair size 10 needles

Tape measure

Scissors

Yarn needle

TECHNIQUES

Binding off, *page 112*

Casting on, *page 108*

Knitting slip stitch, *page 124*

Weaving in loose ends, *page 113*

FINISHED DIMENSIONS

approximately 1 inch wide (rolled) and 60 inches long (without fringe)

06. Repeat steps 2 through 5 for stitch pattern until belt measures 60 inches from the cast-on edge, ending after working step 3 or 5.

07. Bind off on a purl row. Weave in and trim loose ends.

08. Cut six 16-inch strands from extra yarn, fold in half, and tie 3 to each edge of belt for fringe. Knot each fringe end.

IMPROVISATION IDEA

You could also make a superthin summer scarf with this pattern. Cast on 13 stitches for a slightly thicker snake (or leave as is at 7), then work as for belt.

YARN CREDIT

Karabella Yarns "Softig,"
100% cotton, 100-gram ball
(88 yards).
Color: #107

should be about 3½ stitches per inch in the stitch pattern on size 10½ needles. Adjust needle size if necessary to obtain correct gauge. Exact gauge is not critical for this project.

YOU WILL NEED

2 skeins (100 grams each) bulky wool

1 pair size 10½ needles, straight or circular (to knit flat)

2 size 9 double-pointed needles (for I-cord shoulder strap)

Tape measure

Scissors

Yarn needle

Piece of fabric, approximately 30 inches by 8½ inches (optional: for lining)

Sewing needle (optional: for lining)

Sewing thread to match bag (optional: for lining)

bag messenger

This is a slightly smaller, dressier version of the old classic. Knitting three times through one stitch creates lines of big bumps and gives the bag a bit of extra pizzazz. If you wish, you can also add a bright lining to keep those odds and ends secure and to add a splash of color.

BAG

01. Cast 28 stitches on a size 10½ needle, leaving a 6-inch tail to weave in later.

02. Row 1: Purl *(right side)*.

03. Row 2: * *(Knit 1, purl 1, knit 1)* all in 1 stitch *(creating 3 stitches where 1 once was)*. Purl next 3 stitches together. Repeat from * to end of row.

04. Row 3: Purl.

05. Row 4: * Purl 3 stitches together. *(Knit 1, purl 1, knit 1)* all in 1 stitch. Repeat from * to end of row.

06. Repeat steps 2 through 5 for stitch pattern until bag measures 30 inches from the cast-on edge, ending with step 2 or 4.

07. Bind off.

08. Assemble the bag: Be sure that the bound-off end *(which has a slight bias that you can easily correct while seaming the bag)* is on the inside, under the flap when folding. If you will be lining the bag, measure the finished rectangle before assembling the bag.

09. Fold the bag with wrong side facing in, leaving a 7-inch closing flap as pictured. The main part of the bag will be 11½ inches high by 8 inches wide. If you want a longer or shorter flap, adjust it accordingly.

Continued

TECHNIQUES

Binding off, *page 112*

Casting on, *page 108*

Knitting/Purling three times in one stitch

Making and inserting a cloth lining (optional)

Making I-cord

Making seams, *page 120*

Purling three stitches together

Weaving in loose ends, *page 113*

FINISHED DIMENSIONS

approximately 8 inches wide by 30 inches long, assembled to a bag 8 inches wide by 11½ inches long with a 7-inch flap

---

10. Seam the sides of the bag. Weave in and trim loose ends.

11. *Optional lining:* Make a cloth rectangle that is about ½ inch narrower and shorter than your knitted rectangle. Fold and seam as for bag. Drop lining into bag, and baste in place by hand, using matching thread and a sewing needle.

I-CORD SHOULDER STRAP

01. Cast 5 stitches on a size 9 double-pointed needle, leaving an 8-inch tail to join to bag later.

02. Knit 1 row.

03. Slide the stitches to the opposite end of the needle. Shift needle to left hand and knit across again in the same direction, bringing the yarn firmly around behind the stitches to work this row.

04. Repeat step 3 until strap measures 30 inches long from the cast-on edge.

05. Bind off and cut yarn, leaving an 8-inch tail. Sew to bag under the flap.

06. Weave in and trim loose ends.

IMPROVISATION IDEA

Use your favorite stitch pattern in lieu of the trinity stitch above. This is a good project to try in different stitch patterns, as its shape is so simple.

YARN CREDIT

Reynolds "Lopi," 100% Icelandic wool, 100-gram ball *(110 yards).*
Color: #9705

wrist warmers ribby

Fun, fashionable, and supercozy, wrist warmers leave your fingers free to drive or knit while keeping the rest of your forearms warm. The ribbed pattern means that they will turn out especially snug.

01. Cast 22 stitches on a double-pointed needle, leaving a 6-inch tail to weave in later. Divide stitches evenly among 3 needles.

02. Join, being careful not to twist the stitches. Place marker for the beginning of the round.

03. Round 1: Knit.

04. Round 2: * Knit 1, purl 1. Repeat from * to end of round.

05. Repeat steps 3 and 4 for stitch pattern until piece measures 9 inches from the cast-on edge. Make sure you end with round 2 *(step 4)*.

06. Slip first 4 stitches to a small stitch holder. These are being set aside for the thumb. Cast on 2 new stitches. Join new round.

07. Work another 1¼ inches in stitch pattern, ending with a knit round *(step 3)*.

08. Bind off purlwise.

09. Return to the thumb. Slip 4 stitches from holder to a needle. Pick up 4 stitches with your other 2 needles—8 stitches total.

10. Knit 1 round.

Continued

GAUGE

should be about 3 stitches per inch in stitch pattern on size 9 needles. Adjust needle size if necessary to obtain correct gauge.

YOU WILL NEED

1 skein (4 ounces) bulky wool

4 size 9 double-pointed needles

Stitch marker

Tape measure

Scissors

Yarn needle

Small stitch holder

TECHNIQUES

Binding off, *page 112*

Casting on, *page 108*

Knitting in the round, *page 119*

Picking up stitches, *page 122*

Weaving in loose ends, *page 113*

11. * Knit 1, purl 1. Repeat from * to end of round.

12. Knit 1 round.

13. Bind off purlwise.

14. Weave in and trim loose ends.

IMPROVISATION IDEA

This is a good project for experimenting with different yarns. Choose a sport or DK weight yarn *(see page 13)* and try an open work pattern up the wrist or work in stockinette *(see page 115)* using a fun, fuzzy novelty yarn.

YARN CREDIT

Brown Sheep Company "Lamb's Pride Bulky," 85% wool, 15% mohair, 4-ounce skein *(125 yards)*.
Color: #M-102 Orchid Thistle

FINISHED DIMENSIONS

approximately 7½ inches in circumference and 10½ inches long

should be about 2¼ stitches per inch in stockinette stitch on size 11 needles. Adjust needle size if necessary to obtain correct gauge.

YOU WILL NEED

1 skein (4 ounces) bulky yarn

1 pair size 13 needles, straight or circular (to knit flat)

4 size 11 double-pointed needles

Tape measure

Scissors

Yarn needle

Small stitch holder

TECHNIQUES

Casting on, *page 108*

Decreasing, *page 117*

Increasing, *page 116*

Joining a new strand of yarn, *page 114*

Knitting in the round, *page 119*

Making seams, *page 120*

mittens gauntlet

Add a little flair to bulky mittens with a woven cuff. It may take a few rounds to get into the groove of the weave, but once you've got the hang of it you'll want to try this edging out on all sorts of projects. It's a nice, no-sweat variation that adds a bit of visual interest.

01. Cast 30 stitches on a size 13 needle, leaving a 10-inch tail that you will use to seam the cuff later. You will be working the cuff of the mitten flat *(back and forth)*.

02. Row 1: * Knit the second stitch from the back, then knit the first stitch from the front. Let both stitches drop off the needle. Repeat from * until end of row.

03. Row 2: Purl 1, * purl the second stitch and then the first stitch. Let both stitches drop off the needle. Repeat from * until 1 stitch remains. Purl the remaining stitch.

04. Repeat steps 2 and 3 until cuff measures 4 inches from the cast-on edge. End on a knit row *(step 2)*.

05. Divide stitches evenly on 3 size 11 double-pointed needles. You will now be knitting in the round.

06. Join round, being careful that the stitches are not twisted. Knit 1 round, decreasing 10 stitches evenly around—a total of 20 stitches remain.

Continued

Picking up stitches, *page 122*

Stockinette stitch, *page 115*

Weaving in loose ends, *page 113*

Woven stitch

FINISHED DIMENSIONS

approximately 8 inches long by 8 inches around hand; cuff measures 4 inches high by 9 inches around

07. Work 4 rounds even.

08. Increase round for thumb: Increase 1 in the first stitch, then knit around until 1 stitch remains. Increase 1—22 stitches total.

09. Knit 1 round even.

10. Repeat step 8, increasing 2 stitches—24 stitches total.

11. Knit 2 rounds even.

12. Next round: Knit until 3 stitches remain. Place next 6 stitches on stitch holder for thumb; cast on 2 additional stitches—20 stitches remain.

13. Work even for 3½ inches more.

14. Decrease for top of mitten: * Knit 2 together, knit 1. Repeat from * around. End with knit 2 together—13 stitches remain.

15. Knit 1 round even.

16. Knit 2 together all around, ending with knit 1—7 stitches remain.

17. Cut yarn, and draw through remaining stitches. Pull tightly to close hole. Fasten off securely inside mitten.

18. Thumb: Pick up 2 stitches from hand, and place 6 stitches from holder evenly on 3 size 11 double-pointed needles—8 stitches.

19. Join new ball of yarn, and knit even until thumb measures 2½ inches.

20. Knit 2 together around—4 stitches remain.

21. Cut yarn, and draw through remaining stitches. Fasten off as for end of mitten.

22. Weave in loose ends. Seam cuff.

23. Make mitten number 2.

Cast only 20 stitches on the size 13 needle and work the entire cuff in stockinette stitch for a more traditional take on the mittens.

YARN CREDIT

Morehouse Merino "Bulky," 100% merino wool, 4-ounce skein *(102 yards)*.
Color: Periwinkle

apparel

GAUGE

should be about 1.7 stitches per inch in stitch pattern on size 15 needles. Adjust needle size if necessary to obtain correct gauge.

YOU WILL NEED

2 (3, 4, 5) skeins (100 grams each) bulky wool or acrylic

1 pair size 15 needles, straight or circular (to work flat)

Tape measure

Scissors

Yarn needle

TECHNIQUES

Binding off, *page 112*

Casting on, *page 108*

Decreasing, *page 117*

Making seams, *page 120*

Weaving in loose ends, *page 113*

Yarn over, *page 118*

poncho ^{lacy}

Worked on big needles with an easy openwork pattern, this poncho can be whipped up in an afternoon. It makes a great birthday gift for a little one. This pattern fits a toddler (from eighteen months to three years). Directions to fit a young child (four to seven), an older child (eight to fifteen), and an adult (sixteen and up) are in parentheses.

01. Cast on 15 *(19, 21, 25)* stitches, leaving a 6-inch tail to weave in later.

02. Row 1: Purl. *(This is the right side of piece.)*

03. Row 2: Purl.

04. Row 3: Knit 2, * yarn over, slip 1, knit 1, pass slipped stitch over. Repeat from * across to last stitch, ending with knit 1.

05. Row 4: Purl.

06. Repeat steps 2 through 5 for stitch pattern until rectangle measures 18 *(22, 26, 30)* inches from the cast-on edge. Bind off loosely.

07. Knit a second rectangle.

Continued

FINISHED DIMENSIONS

Toddler: 2 rectangles, 9 inches wide by 18 inches long

Young child: 2 rectangles, 11 inches wide by 22 inches long

Older child: 2 rectangles, 13 inches wide by 26 inches long

Adult: 2 rectangles, 15 inches wide by 30 inches long

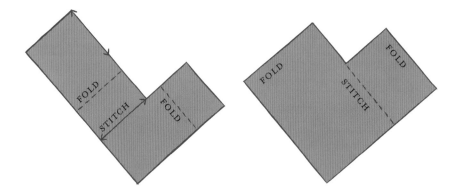

08. Assemble poncho. Place the cast-on edge of rectangle 1 against the lower side of rectangle 2. The cast-on rows will create a 90-degree angle. Seam rectangle 1 to rectangle 2. The point at the bottom is the middle of the poncho. Fold the rectangles over and seam the bind-off edge of rectangle 2 to the side of rectangle 1.

09. Weave in and trim loose ends.

IMPROVISATION IDEA

You can use any stitch pattern and combination of colors to create a fun, fast-to-knit poncho using the dimensions given. Why not try a rainbow-colored poncho in garter stitch *(see page 115)* next?

YARN CREDIT

Reynolds Yarns "Blizzard," 65% alpaca, 35% acrylic, 100-gram ball *(66 yards).*
Color: #641

capelet ^{fuzzy}

This adorable fuzzy cloak buttons at the top and falls away to skim the elbows. Worked in garter stitch on big needles, the weave is loose enough so you don't have to make a buttonhole. This pattern fits an extra-small woman (28- to 30-inch chest). Directions to fit small to medium (32–34) and medium to large (36–38) are in parentheses.

01. With yarn held double *(see page 129)*, cast on 34 *(38, 42)* stitches for neck edge, leaving a 6-inch tail to weave in later.

02. Row 1: Knit 7 *(8, 9)*, place first marker, knit 2, place second marker, knit 16 *(18, 20)*, place third marker, knit 2, place fourth marker, knit remaining 7 *(8, 9)* stitches.

03. Rows 2–4: Knit.

04. Row 5 *(increase row)*: Knit to 1 stitch before first marker, increase 1. Slip marker, increase 1. Knit to 1 stitch before second marker, increase 1. Slip second marker, increase 1. Knit to 1 stitch before third marker, increase 1. Slip third marker, increase 1. Knit to 1 stitch before fourth marker, increase 1. Slip fourth marker, increase 1. Knit to end of row—8 stitches increased; 42 *(46, 50)* stitches.

05. Work in garter stitch, repeating increase row every fifth row 5 *(6, 7)* times, a total of 6 *(7, 8)* increase rows—48 *(56, 64)* stitches increased; 82 *(94, 106)* stitches.

06. Work 3 rows even in garter stitch.

07. Row 33 *(38, 43)* *(decrease row)*: Knit 2, knit 2 together; knit across until 4 stitches remain unworked; knit 2 together. End knit 2—2 stitches decreased; 80 *(92, 104)* stitches remain.

Continued

GAUGE

should be about 1½ stitches per inch in garter stitch (knit all stitches, every row) on a size 17 needle. Adjust needle size if necessary to obtain corrected gauge.

YOU WILL NEED

4 (6, 6) skeins (50 grams each) chunky "fun fur"–type yarn

1 size 17 circular needle, 29 inches long (to work flat)

4 stitch markers

Tape measure

Scissors

Yarn needle

Row counter

One 2-inch button

Sewing needle

Sewing thread to match yarn

TECHNIQUES

Binding off, *page 112*

Casting on, *page 108*

Decreasing, *page 117*

Garter stitch, *page 115*

Increasing, *page 116*

Sewing on buttons

Weaving in loose ends, *page 113*

FINISHED DIMENSIONS

approximately 12 inches long
by 23 (25, 28) inches wide at
neck edge; note that the fabric
is very flexible

08. Row 34 *(39, 44)*: Work even.

09. Row 35 *(40, 45)*: Repeat step 7, decreasing 2 more stitches—a total of 4 stitches decreased; 78 *(90, 102)* stitches remain.

10. Row 36 *(41, 46) (decrease row)*: Knit 1, knit 2 together. Knit until 3 stitches remain. Knit 2 together. End knit 1—2 stitches decreased; 76 *(88, 100)* stitches remain.

11. Bind off. Weave in and trim loose ends.

12. Sew a big button at the top of the capelet.

IMPROVISATION IDEA

Instead of a button, make ties with pom-poms at the end.

Directions for pom-poms:
Cut 2 circular pieces of cardboard the size you'd like your pom-poms to be. Cut a thin, pie-shaped wedge into the circles, starting at the outer edge and ending in the center of each circle, then use the wedge as an entry point to snip a smaller circle in the center of the big circles. Wind yarn very tightly around the cardboard, using the wedge to guide the yarn into the inner circle. Have a long piece of yarn ready to tie up the pom-pom. Use very sharp scissors to snip the yarn between the 2 circles. Hold tightly onto the yarn to make sure it doesn't slip away. Guide the long piece of yarn into the center of the small circle, then ease out the 2 pieces of cardboard. Quickly draw the long piece of yarn tightly around the smaller pieces and secure. You can use the longer piece of the yarn to tie the pom-pom to your capelet. Trim pom-poms if necessary.

YARN CREDIT

Berroco "Softy," 52% DuPont Tactel nylon, 48% nylon, 50-gram ball *(96 meters)*.
Color: #2901

shrug ^{simple}

This very easy shrug is worked entirely in stockinette stitch. It's made of springy cotton tape and is formfitting, with bells at the wrist. It's the ideal summer accessory. Slip it on when you're inside in air conditioning and then slip it off and throw it in your purse when you're out in the warm air.

01. Cast on 33 stitches, leaving a 6-inch tail to weave in later.

02. Work 3 inches even in stockinette stitch.

03. Decrease row: Continuing in stockinette stitch, bind off first stitch; work until 2 stitches remain, then knit (or purl if you are on a purl row), the final 2 stitches together—2 stitches decreased.

04. Continue to work in stockinette stitch, repeating the decrease row when sleeve measures 4½ inches from the beginning and again when sleeve measures 5½ inches—you are now working on 27 stitches.

05. Work even for 6½ inches until sleeve measures 12 inches from the cast-on edge.

06. Increase row: Increase 1 stitch each end of this row by knitting (or purling) twice in the second stitch and in the next-to-last stitch of the row—2 stitches increased; 29 stitches.

07. Repeat increase row 3 more times, when sleeve measures 13½ inches, 15 inches, and 16 inches from the cast-on edge—35 stitches total.

08. Work even for 23 more inches; your entire shrug will measure 39 inches from the cast-on edge thus far.

Continued

APPAREL

GAUGE

should be about 3 stitches per inch in stockinette stitch on size 11 needles. Adjust needle size if necessary to obtain correct gauge.

YOU WILL NEED

5 skeins (50 grams each) cotton tape

1 pair size 11 needles, straight or circular (to knit flat)

Tape measure

Scissors

Yarn needle

TECHNIQUES

Binding off, *page 112*

Casting on, *page 108*

Decreasing, *page 117*

Increasing, *page 116*

Making seams, *page 120*

Stockinette stitch, *page 115*

Weaving in loose ends, *page 113*

FINISHED DIMENSIONS

approximately 55 inches long
and 10 inches wide at back,
partially unrolled

09. Repeat decrease row *(step 3)* 4 times, when shrug measures 39 inches, 40 inches, 41½ inches, and 43 inches from the cast-on edge—27 stitches remain.

10. Work even for 6½ inches more; your entire shrug measures 49½ inches from the cast-on edge thus far.

11. Repeat increase row *(step 6)* 3 times, when shrug measures 49½ inches, 50½ inches, and 52 inches from the cast-on edge—33 stitches total.

12. Work even in stockinette stitch for 3 inches; your entire shrug measures 55 inches from the cast-on edge. Bind off.

13. Create sleeves by seaming shrug to 19 inches from wrist edge to underarm on each side. Weave in and trim loose ends.

14. When you put the shrug on, give it a tug at the back to unroll, and shape the top roll around your shoulders.

IMPROVISATION IDEA

Shrugs are nice for experimenting with different yarns and stitch patterns. You could try a thinner yarn with a nice openwork pattern for a delicate, lacy look or a thicker handcrafted yarn for a chunky counterpart to a tank top. If you are experimenting with a different sleeve shape, work the shrug on a circular needle so you can try it on as you go along.

YARN CREDIT

Rowan "Cotton Tape," 100% cotton, 50-gram ball *(65 meters)*.
Color: #557

shawl _sea foam_

Wispy yarns and delicate colors create a light, luxurious summer shawl. Because you'll be knitting thinner yarns on big needles, the weave will be ultra-loose. It works up very quickly. This shawl just covers the shoulders and is secured with ties that you'll add at the end of the project.

01. Cast on 3 stitches with yarn A, leaving a 6-inch tail to weave in later.

02. Knit 1 row.

03. Knit 1, increase 1, knit 1—4 stitches total.

04. Knit 1 row even.

05. Knit 1, increase 1 in each of the next 2 stitches, end knit 1—6 stitches total.

06. Let yarn A rest. Join yarn B, and knit 1 row even.

07. Increase row: With yarn B, knit 1, increase 1, knit until 2 stitches remain, increase 1. End knit 1—8 stitches total.

08. With yarns A and B held together, knit 4 rows, increasing in the second and next-to-last stitches on the second and fourth rows as in step 7. Cut yarn A, leaving a 6-inch tail to weave in later.

09. With yarn B alone, knit 4 rows, increasing in the second and next-to-last stitches on the second and fourth rows as in step 7. Join yarn C. Cut yarn B, leaving a 6-inch tail to weave in later.

Continued

GAUGE

should be about 2 stitches per inch in garter stitch on a size 15 needle. Adjust needle size if necessary to obtain correct gauge.

YOU WILL NEED

1 skein (50 grams) worsted weight novelty yarn, yarn A

1 skein (50 grams) mohair, yarn B

1 skein (50 grams) worsted weight silk-alpaca blend, yarn C

1 size 15 circular needle, 32 inches long (to knit flat)

Tape measure

Scissors

Yarn needle

TECHNIQUES

Binding off, _page 112_

Casting on, _page 108_

Garter stitch, _page 115_

Increasing, _page 116_

Joining a new strand of yarn, _page 114_

Picking up stitches, *page 122*

Weaving in loose ends, *page 113*

Yarn double, *page 129*

FINISHED DIMENSIONS

approximately 22 inches long and
52 inches wide at top, including
4-inch ties

10. Knit 6 rows with C, increasing in the second and next-to-last stitches on the second, fourth, and sixth rows. Join yarn A. Cut yarn C, leaving a 6-inch tail to weave in later.

11. Knit 4 rows, increasing in the second and next-to-last stitches on the second and fourth rows.

12. Repeat steps 6 through 11 two more times. Your shawl should measure 22 inches from the starting point to the top.

13. Bind off loosely. Cut yarn, leaving a 6-inch tail to weave in later.

14. Create ties: Pick up 4 stitches from the edge of your final yarn A stripe. Join yarn A, and work 4 inches in garter stitch. Bind off. Cut yarn. Repeat on the other side of the stripe.

15. Weave in and trim loose ends.

IMPROVISATION IDEA

Make the shawl into a rectangular wrap. Cast on 32 stitches, and knit until the wrap measures 80 inches long. You will need extra yarn for this, approximately 2 skeins of each type.

YARN CREDIT

GGH "Esprit," 100% nylon, 50-gram ball *(80 meters)*.
Color: #22

Classic Elite "La Gran Mohair," 76.5% mohair, 17.5% wool, 6% nylon, 1½-ounce skein *(90 yards)*.
Color: #6572 Underappreciated Green

Debbie Bliss "Alpaca Silk," 80% baby alpaca, 20% silk, 50-gram ball *(50 meters)*.
Color: #25002

should be about 2.6 stitches per inch and 4 rows per inch in stockinette stitch on a size 10½ needle. Adjust needle size if necessary to obtain correct gauge.

YOU WILL NEED

6 (6, 7, 7, 8) skeins (50 grams each) bulky wool

1 size 10½ circular needle, 29 inches long

1 size 10½ crochet hook

2 stitch markers

Tape measure

Scissors

Yarn needle

Large stitch holder

TECHNIQUES

Binding off, *page 112*

Casting on, *page 108*

Crocheting slip stitch, *page 125*

vest ॰ scoop neck

You'll give an otherwise dull (or overworn) shirt a new life when you throw this Scoop Neck Vest on top. It's sized to be formfitting, so if you prefer a looser fit, knit the next size up. In the interest of speed, the vest is knit in the round until you reach the armholes, then the front and back are worked separately. This pattern fits a small woman (32-inch chest). Directions to fit chest sizes 34, 36, 38, and 40 inches are in parentheses.

01. Cast 82 *(88, 94, 100, 106)* stitches on your 29-inch needle, leaving a 6-inch tail to weave in later. Place marker. Join round, being careful not to twist the stitches.

02. Round 1: Work in knit 1, purl 1 ribbing, placing second marker at midround, after stitch 41 *(44, 47, 50, 53)*.

03. Work 5 inches in knit 1, purl 1 ribbing.

04. Work in stockinette stitch *(knit all stitches, every round)* for 8 *(9, 10, 11, 12)* additional inches until piece measures 13 *(14, 15, 16, 17)* inches from cast-on edge.

05. Divide for armholes: Place the 41 *(44, 47, 50, 53)* stitches between markers 2 and 1 onto large stitch holder. You will work these later for the back.

06. Shape the armholes: Continuing in stockinette stitch *(knit on right side, purl on wrong side)*, bind off 3 stitches at the beginning of the next 2 rows. Bind off 2 stitches at the beginning of the next 2 rows. Bind off 1 stitch at the beginning of the next 2 *(4, 4, 6, 6)* rows—12 *(14, 14, 16, 16)* stitches

Continued

total bound off for armholes; 29 *(30, 33, 34, 37)* stitches remain. End with a wrong-side row.

07. Shape neck *(right side)*: Work 10 *(10, 11, 11, 12)* stitches; join a second ball of yarn, and bind off 9 *(10, 11, 12, 13)* center stitches; work to end—10 *(10, 11, 11, 12)* stitches each shoulder.

08. Working both sides at same time, at each neck edge, decrease 1 stitch every other row 4 *(4, 4, 4, 4)* times—a total of 17 *(18, 19, 20, 21)* stitches bound off for neck; 6 *(6, 7, 7, 8)* stitches remain for each shoulder.

09. Work even until piece measures 18½ *(20, 21½, 23, 24½)* inches from cast-on edge—armhole measures 5½ *(6, 6½, 7, 7½)* inches from dividing row. End with a purl row. Bind off.

10. Work the back: Move the stitches for the back from the stitch holder to your needle.

11. Repeat step 6.

12. Work even in stockinette stitch until piece measures 16 *(17½, 19, 20½, 22)* inches. End with a purl row.

13. Shape neck *(right side)*: Work 7 *(7, 8, 8, 9)* stitches; join a second ball of yarn, and bind off 15 *(16, 17, 18, 19)* center stitches; work to end—7 *(7, 8, 8, 9)* stitches remain for each shoulder.

14. Working both sides at same time, at each neck edge, decrease 1 stitch every other row once, a total of 17 *(18, 19, 20, 21)* stitches bound off for neck—6 *(6, 7, 7, 8)* stitches remain for each shoulder.

15. Work even until piece measures 18½ *(20, 21½, 23, 24½)* inches from cast-on edge. End with a purl row. Bind off.

16. Using your yarn needle, seam shoulders. Weave in and trim loose ends.

17. Using your crochet hook, join a new piece of yarn, and edge neck and arm-holes in slip stitch for a more finished look. Weave in and trim loose ends.

front

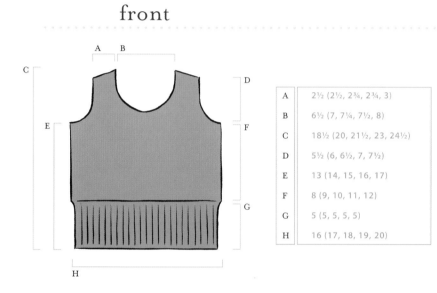

A	2½ (2½, 2¾, 2¾, 3)
B	6½ (7, 7¼, 7½, 8)
C	18½ (20, 21½, 23, 24½)
D	5½ (6, 6½, 7, 7½)
E	13 (14, 15, 16, 17)
F	8 (9, 10, 11, 12)
G	5 (5, 5, 5, 5)
H	16 (17, 18, 19, 20)

IMPROVISATION IDEA

For a more shallow, squarer neck, knit front and back following instructions for back neck.

YARN CREDIT

Debbie Bliss "Merino Chunky," 100% merino wool, 50-gram ball *(50 meters)*. **Color:** #140614

GAUGE

should be about 2½ stitches per inch and 4 rows per inch in stockinette stitch on a size 9 needle. Adjust needle size if necessary to obtain correct gauge.

YOU WILL NEED

5 (5, 6) skeins (1½ ounces each) heavy worsted weight mohair

1 size 9 circular needle, 24 inches long

Tape measure

Scissors

Yarn needle

Row counter

Stitch holder

TECHNIQUES

Binding off, *page 112*

Casting on, *page 108*

Decreasing, *page 117*

Increasing, *page 116*

Joining a new strand of yarn, *page 114*

ballet sweater fuzzy

Instead of the usual shawl, why not wear a fun and fuzzy ballet sweater over that sleeveless or short-sleeved dress? The three-quarter-length sleeves give it a dressier feel, and the dramatic ties make the fit more flexible. This pattern fits a small to medium woman (30- to 34-inch chest). Directions to fit medium to large (36–40) and large to extra large (42–44) are in parentheses. There is a certain amount of give in the sizing, due to the overlap of the right and left fronts of the sweater.

BACK

01. Cast 36 *(40, 46)* stitches on your needle, leaving a 6-inch tail to weave in later.

02. Work 4 rows in stockinette stitch, ending with a purl *(wrong-side)* row.

03. Row 5 *(increase row)*: Knit 1, increase 1, knit until 2 stitches remain, increase 1, end knit 1—38 *(42, 48)* stitches total.

04. Continue working in stockinette stitch, repeating increase row 1 *(2, 2)* more time in row 15 for the smaller size and in rows 15 and 25 for the larger sizes—40 *(46, 52)* stitches total. Work even until piece measures 6½ *(7½, 8½)* inches from cast-on edge. End with a purl row

05. Shape armholes: Bind off 2 stitches at the beginning of the next 2 rows. Bind off 1 stitch at the beginning of the next 4 rows—8 stitches total reduced for all sizes; 32 *(38, 44)* stitches remain.

Continued

Making seams, *page 120*

Stockinette stitch, *page 115*

Weaving in loose ends, *page 113*

FINISHING

Using your yarn needle and extra mohair, seam shoulders. Set in sleeves. Seam sleeves. Seam sides. Sew ties to the left and right fronts of the garment as pictured, placing the bottom of the tie even with the base of the garment and the top approximately 2¾ inches above. Weave in and trim all loose ends.

06. Work even until armholes measure 7 *(7½, 8)* inches from beginning of shaping, ending with a purl row.

07. Shape the neck (right side): Work 8 *(10, 12)* stitches; join a second ball of yarn, and bind off 16 *(18, 20)* center stitches; work to end—8 *(10, 12)* stitches each shoulder.

08. Shape shoulders: Working both sides at same time, at each armhole edge, bind off 4 *(5, 6)* stitches every other row 2 times, no stitches remaining to bind off.

LEFT FRONT

01. Cast on 22 *(25, 28)* stitches, leaving a 6-inch tail to weave in later. Work 4 rows in stockinette stitch, ending with a purl *(wrong-side)* row.

02. Row 5 *(increase row)*: Knit 1, increase 1, knit to end.

03. Rows 6–9: Work even in stockinette stitch for 4 rows—piece measures approximately 2 inches from cast-on edge. End with a knit *(right-side)* row at center front edge.

04. Begin shaping the collar *(decrease row)*: Purl 1, slip 1, purl 1, pass slipped stitch over, purl to end. Work 3 rows even.

05. Repeat step 4 a total of 12 *(14, 15)* times. At the same time, repeat increase row *(step 2)* at side edge *(beginning of right-side rows)* 1 *(2, 2)* more time in row 15 for the smaller size and in rows 15 and 25 for the larger sizes—2 *(3, 3)* stitches increased in total.

06. Continuing collar shaping as established, shape armhole at 6½ *(7½ , 8½)* inches. When collar shaping is complete, work even on the remaining 8 *(10, 12)* shoulder stitches until piece measures 13½ *(15, 16½)* inches, and then shape shoulders as for back.

RIGHT FRONT

01. Cast on 22 *(25, 28)* stitches, leaving a 6-inch tail to weave in later. Work 4 rows in stockinette stitch, ending with a purl *(wrong-side)* row.

02. Row 5 *(increase row)*: Knit until 2 stitches remain, increase 1, knit remaining stitch.

03. Rows 6–9: Work even in stockinette stitch for 4 rows—piece measures approximately 2 inches from cast-on edge. End with a knit *(right-side)* row at side edge.

04. Begin shaping the collar *(decrease row)*. Purl until 3 stitches remain. Purl 2 together, end purl 1. Work 3 rows even.

05. Repeat step 4 a total of 12 *(14, 15)* times. At the same time, repeat increase row *(step 2)* at side edge *(end of right-side rows)* 1 *(2, 2)* more time in row 15 for the smaller size and in rows 15 and 25 for the larger sizes—2 *(3, 3)* stitches increased in total.

06. Continuing collar shaping as established, shape armhole at 6½ *(7½, 8½)* inches. When collar shaping is complete, work even on the remaining 8 *(10, 12)* shoulder stitches until piece measures 13½ *(15, 16½)* inches, and then shape shoulders as for back.

SLEEVES (MAKE 2)

01. Cast on 29 *(32, 35)* stitches, leaving a 6-inch tail to weave in later.

02. Work 9 *(9½, 10)* inches in stockinette stitch, ending with a purl row.

03. Increase row: Knit 1, increase 1, knit until 2 stitches remain, increase 1, end knit 1—a total of 31 *(34, 37)* stitches.

04. Work 2 more inches in stockinette stitch, then repeat increase row *(step 3)*, once more—33 *(36, 39)* stitches total.

05. Work even until sleeve measures 13½ *(14, 14½)* inches from cast-on edge.

06. Shape sleeve cap: Bind off 3 stitches at the beginning of the next 2 rows, then bind off 1 stitch at the beginning of the next 16 *(18, 20)* rows. Work even on remaining 11 *(12, 13)* stitches until sleeve cap measures 4¾ *(5¼, 5¾)* inches from beginning of shaping. Bind off.

TIES (MAKE 2)

01. Cast on 7 stitches, leaving a 6-inch tail to weave in later.

02. Work in stockinette stitch until tie measures 42 inches from cast-on edge.

03. Bind off.

back

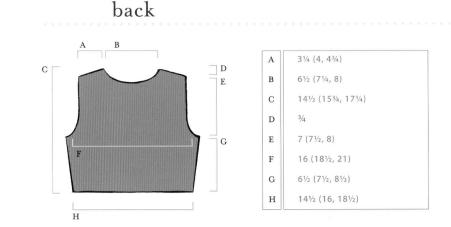

A	3¼ (4, 4¾)
B	6½ (7¼, 8)
C	14½ (15¾, 17¼)
D	¾
E	7 (7½, 8)
F	16 (18½, 21)
G	6½ (7½, 8½)
H	14½ (16, 18½)

left front

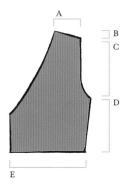

A	3¼ (4, 4¾)
B	¾
C	7 (7½, 8)
D	6½ (7½, 8½)
E	9 (10, 11)

sleeve

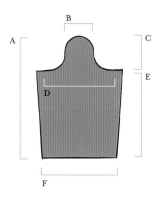

A	18¼ (19¼, 20¼)
B	4¼ (4½, 4¾)
C	4¾ (5¼, 5¾)
D	13¼ (14½, 15½)
E	13½ (14, 14½)
F	11½ (12¾, 14)

summer shift cap-sleeved

Throw this light, sunny dress on over a swimsuit or pants. Or if you're more daring, wear it over a slip! Worked double stranded on size 13 needles, it is quite possible to finish in a day. This pattern fits an extra-small woman (28- to 30-inch chest). Directions to fit small (32–34), medium (36–38), large (40), and extra large (42) are in parentheses.

01. With yarn held double, cast 88 *(94, 100, 106, 112)* stitches on your 29-inch needle, leaving a 6-inch tail to weave in later. Place marker. Join round, being careful not to twist the stitches.

02. Round 1: Knit, placing second marker at midround, after stitch 44 *(47, 50, 53, 56)*.

03. Round 2: Purl.

04. Rounds 3 and 4: Knit.

05. Round 5 *(decrease round)*: Slip first marker. Slip 1, knit 1, pass slipped stitch over. Knit to second marker. Slip marker. Knit 2 together. Knit to end of round—2 stitches decreased; 86 *(92, 98, 104, 110)* stitches remain.

06. Continue in stockinette stitch, decreasing every 5 rounds 4 more times *(total of 5 decrease rounds; 10 stitches decreased)*, then every 4 rounds 9 times *(total of 14 decrease rounds, 28 stitches decreased)*. You now have 60 *(66, 72, 78, 84)* stitches remaining.

07. Work even in stockinette stitch until dress measures 23 *(24, 25, 26, 27)* inches from cast-on edge.

08. Shaping the armholes: You will now be working flat *(back and forth)* on the back and then the front. You can place the stitches from the front on a large

Continued

GAUGE

should be about 2 stitches per inch in stockinette stitch on a size 13 needle. Adjust needle size if necessary to obtain correct gauge.

YOU WILL NEED

6 (6, 6, 8, 8) skeins (100 grams each) worsted weight cotton or cotton blend yarn

1 size 13 circular needle, 29 inches long

1 size 13 circular needle, 16 inches long

2 stitch markers

Tape measure

Scissors

Yarn needle

Row counter

Large stitch holder (optional)

TECHNIQUES

Binding off, *page 112*

Casting on, *page 108*

stitch holder or just leave them on the longer needle and work the back with the short one—30 *(33, 36, 39, 42)* stitches each for the back and front.

09. Bind off 3 stitches at the beginning of the next 2 rows—24 *(27, 30, 33, 36)* stitches remain for back.

10. Work 2 rows even in stockinette stitch.

11. Bind off 2 stitches at the beginning of the next 2 rows—20 *(23, 26, 29, 32)* stitches remain.

12. Work 1 row even.

13. Bind off 1 stitch at both sides of the same row—18 *(21, 24, 27, 30)* stitches remain.

14. Work 1 row even.

15. Repeat steps 13 and 14 until 14 *(17, 18, 19, 20)* stitches remain, ending with step 14.

16. Bind off.

17. Repeat steps 9 through 16 for the front. *(You will have to join a new yarn double strand.)*

18. Creating the sleeves: With right side facing and using your 16-inch needle, pick up and knit 18 *(20, 20, 22, 22)* stitches, 9 *(10, 10, 11, 11)* from each side of the armhole. Cast on 9 *(10, 11, 12, 12)* stitches. The cast-on stitches will form the top of your sleeve.

19. Place marker, join, and work 3 rounds in stockinette stitch, placing a second marker at the beginning of the cast-on stitches.

20. Knit short rows to shape the cap sleeve: You will be working flat to create the cap. Turn work and purl back to second marker.

21. Turn, knit to 1 stitch past first marker.

22. Turn, purl to 1 stitch past second marker.

23. Turn, knit to 2 stitches past first marker.

24. Turn, purl to 2 stitches past second marker.

25. Turn, knit to 3 stitches past first marker.

26. Turn, purl to 3 stitches past second marker.

27. Turn, knit to 4 stitches past first marker.

28. Turn, purl to 4 stitches past second marker.

29. Turn, knit to 5 stitches past first marker.

30. Turn, purl to 5 stitches past second marker.

31. Knit completely around sleeve, passing both short end edges and ending at center of underarm. Ending at the underarm will make it easier to hide your loose tail of yarn after you bind off.

32. Bind off. Weave in loose ends and trim.

front

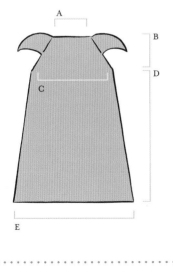

A	7 (8½, 9, 9½, 10)
B	6¼ (6¼, 7, 7¾, 8½)
C	15 (16½, 18, 19½, 21)
D	23 (24, 25, 26, 27)
E	22 (23½, 25, 26½, 28)

IMPROVISATION IDEA

Use wool instead of cotton to knit a sweater alternative to wear over pants.

YARN CREDIT

Blue Sky Alpacas "Blue Sky Cotton," 100% cotton, 100-gram ball *(150 yards)*.
Color: #608

should be about 1¾ stitches per inch in stockinette stitch on a size 13 needle. Adjust needle size if necessary to obtain correct gauge.

YOU WILL NEED

4 (5, 6, 7) skeins (8 ounces each) superbulky wool

1 size 13 circular needle, 29 inches long

1 size 13 circular needle, 16 inches long

1 stitch marker

Tape measure

Scissors

Yarn needle

Large stitch holder

TECHNIQUES

Binding off, *page 112*

Blocking (*optional*), *page 124*

Casting on, *page 108*

Decreasing, *page 117*

pullover men's crew neck

This bulky, oversized sweater knits up in a flash. This pattern fits an extra-small man (38- to 40-inch chest). Directions to fit small (42–44), medium (46–48), and large (50–52) are in parentheses.

01. Cast 74 *(80, 88, 94)* stitches on your 29-inch circular needle, leaving a 6-inch tail to weave in later. Place marker and join, being careful not to twist the stitches.

02. Work 2 *(2½, 3, 3)* inches in knit 1, purl 1 ribbing.

03. Change to stockinette stitch. Work even until piece measures 15½ *(16½, 17½, 18½)* inches from cast-on edge.

04. Place 37 *(40, 44, 47)* stitches for the front on large stitch holder. You will now be working flat to the shoulders.

05. Finishing the back: Work 9½ *(10, 10½, 11)* more inches in stockinette stitch—25 *(26½, 28, 29½)* inches total. End with a wrong-side row. Bind off.

06. Return to front. Work 7 *(7, 7½, 8)* inches in stockinette stitch. End with a wrong-side row.

07. Shape neck *(right side)*: Knit 17 *(18, 20, 21)* stitches. Join a second ball of yarn, and bind off 3 *(4, 4, 5)* center stitches. Knit 17 *(18, 20, 21)* stitches to end—17 *(18, 20, 21)* stitches per shoulder.

08. Working both sides at the same time, at each neck edge, bind off 2 stitches every other row once—7 *(8, 8, 9)* stitches total for neck, then 1 stitch at each neck edge 2 *(2, 3, 3)* times—11 *(12, 14, 15)* stitches total for neck; 13 *(14, 15, 16)*

Continued

stitches remain for each shoulder. Work even until the front measures the same as the back to the top of the shoulders, ending with a wrong-side row. Bind off.

09. Create sleeves: Cast 18 *(19, 20, 20)* stitches on your 29-inch needle *(you will be working flat)*. Work 2 *(2½, 3, 3)* inches in knit 1, purl 1 ribbing.

10. Knit 1 row.

11. Purl 1 row.

12. Increase row: Knit 1, increase 1, knit until 2 stitches remain, increase 1, knit 1—2 stitches increased.

13. Continue working in stockinette stitch, repeating increase row *(step 12)* every fourth row 3 *(3, 4, 5)* more times—a total of 8 *(8, 10, 12)* stitches increased; 26 *(27, 30, 32)* stitches.

14. Continue in stockinette stitch, repeating increase row every sixth row 4 *(4, 3, 3)* times—a total of 16 *(16, 16, 18)* stitches increased; 34 *(35, 36, 38)* stitches total.

15. Work even in stockinette stitch until sleeve measures 18 *(18½, 19, 19½)* inches, ending with a wrong-side row.

16. Bind off. Make second sleeve.

17. Finishing: Using your yarn needle and extra yarn, sew shoulder seams. Set in sleeves, and sew sleeve seams.

18. Crewneck: Using your 16-inch circular needle and with right side facing, pick up and knit 11 *(14, 14, 15)* stitches from back, 2 *(2, 2, 2)* stitches from first shoulder, 13 *(14, 14, 15)* stitches from front, and 2 *(2, 2, 2)* stitches from second shoulder—28 *(32, 32, 34)* stitches total. Place stitch marker and join.

19. Work 3 *(4, 4, 5)* rounds in knit 1, purl 1 rib.

20. Bind off loosely in pattern. Weave in and trim loose ends. Block if desired.

front

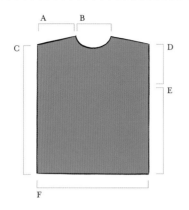
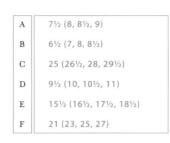

A	7½ (8, 8½, 9)
B	6½ (7, 8, 8½)
C	25 (26½, 28, 29½)
D	9½ (10, 10½, 11)
E	15½ (16½, 17½, 18½)
F	21 (23, 25, 27)

sleeve

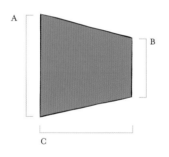

A	19 (20, 21, 22)
B	10¼ (11½, 11½, 11½)
C	18 (18½, 19, 19½)

IMPROVISATION IDEA

The men's small can become
a women's medium sweater and
the men's medium a women's
large. Subtract an inch from the
arm length for a better fit.

YARN CREDIT

Brown Sheep Company "Burly Spun,"
100% wool, 8-ounce skein *(132 yards)*.
Color: #BS-04 Charcoal Heather

GAUGE

should be about 2½ stitches per inch and 4 rows per inch in stockinette stitch on a size 10 needle. Adjust needle size if necessary to obtain correct gauge.

YOU WILL NEED

3 (4, 5, 5, 5, 6) skeins (50 grams each) bulky cotton or cotton-blend yarn

1 size 10 circular needle, 24 inches long

2 size 9 double-pointed needles (for I-cord straps)

2 stitch markers

Tape measure

Scissors

Yarn needle

Large stitch holder

TECHNIQUES

Binding off, *page 112*

Casting on, *page 108*

Decreasing, *page 117*

ribby halter

This halter is so quick to knit, you can make it in the morning to wear to a lunchtime barbecue. You can also adjust the straps to increase (or decrease) the placement of the center V. Being a more modest type, I prefer it at midbust, but if you're a little more daring, let it dip. The ribbing will adjust to fit to your torso and bust. This pattern fits an extra-small woman (30-inch chest). Directions to fit chest sizes 32, 34, 36, 38, and 40 inches are in parentheses.

01. Cast 76 *(80, 84, 88, 96, 100)* stitches on your 24-inch circular needle, leaving a 6-inch tail to weave in later.

02. Place marker and join, being careful not to twist the stitches. Work 9 *(9½, 10, 10½, 11, 11½)* inches in knit 2, purl 2 ribbing.

03. Bind off 32 *(34, 36, 38, 42, 44)* stitches—44 *(46, 48, 50, 54, 56)* stitches remain on your needle. You will be working flat for the rest of the project.

04. Work 2 *(4, 4, 6, 6, 8)* rows in stockinette stitch. End with a purl *(wrong-side)* row.

05. Bind off center 2 stitches. Knit to end of row. You will be working separately on each cup—21 *(22, 23, 24, 26, 27)* stitches. Place stitches for second cup on large stitch holder.

06. Next row: Bind off 1 stitch at armhole edge. Purl across. Place a marker after stitch 9 *(9, 10, 10, 11, 11)* and a marker after stitch 11 *(12, 12, 13, 14, 14)*. Purl to end—20 *(21, 22, 23, 25, 26)* stitches remain.

Continued

FINISHED DIMENSIONS

27 (28½, 30, 31½, 33, 34½) inches at waist in slightly relaxed rib and 30 (32, 34, 36, 38, 40) inches at bust in stockinette stitch

07. Next row *(decrease row)*: Knit to 2 stitches before first marker, slip 1, knit 1, pass slipped stitch over. Knit to second marker, slip marker, knit 2 together, knit to end—2 stitches decreased; 18 *(19, 20, 21, 23, 24)* stitches remain.

08. Purl 1 row.

09. Next row *(decrease row)*: Knit 1, slip 1, knit 1, pass slipped stitch over, knit until 3 stitches remain, knit 2 together, end knit 1—2 stitches decreased; 16 *(17, 18, 19, 21, 22)* stitches remain.

10. Work 3 rows even in stockinette stitch.

11. Next row *(decrease row)*: Knit 1, slip 1, knit 1, pass slipped stitch over. Knit to 2 stitches before first marker, slip 1, knit 1, pass slipped stitch over. Knit to second marker, slip marker, knit 2 together. Knit until 3 stitches remain, knit 2 together, end knit 1—4 stitches decreased; 12 *(13, 14, 15, 17, 18)* stitches remain.

12. Work 3 rows even in stockinette stitch.

13. Repeat step 11 again—8 *(9, 10, 11, 13, 14)* stitches remain.

14. Work 3 rows even in stockinette stitch.

15. Decrease row *(right side)*: Knit 1, slip 1, pass slipped stitch over. Knit until 3 stitches remain, knit 2 together, end knit 1—2 stitches decreased; 6 *(7, 8, 9, 11, 12)* stitches remain.

16. Purl 1 row, removing markers.

17. Continuing in stockinette stitch, repeat step 15 every other row 1 *(2, 2, 3, 4, 4)* time—4 *(3, 4, 3, 3, 4)* stitches remain.

18. All sizes: Purl 1 row.

19. Bind off 1 *(0, 1, 0, 0, 1)* stitch. Knit to end of row.

20. Transfer 3 remaining stitches to a double-pointed needle. Work 20 *(21, 22, 23, 24, 25)* inches of I-cord or to length desired.

21. Bind off. Weave in and trim loose ends.

front

A	15 (16, 17, 18, 19, 20)
B	9 (9½, 10, 10½, 11, 11½)
C	13½ (14¼, 15, 15¾, 16½, 17¼)

IMPROVISATION IDEA

If you want to increase the coverage, knit a few extra inches of ribbing at the bottom.

YARN CREDIT

Lang "Colombo," 53% silk, 47% cotton, 50-gram ball *(50 meters)*.
Color: #0060

gifts to give and get

throw
match my couch

This throw is one of the lengthier projects you'll find in this book. It's not a difficult project, but it is very large. That said, compared to other blanket patterns, this one knits up quite quickly, as you'll be knitting two strands of bulky yarn together as one on size 17 needles.

01. With yarn held double, cast on 80 stitches, leaving a 6-inch tail to weave in later.

02. Knit 1 row.

03. Next row: Slip first stitch as if to purl. Purl across row.

04. Slip first stitch as if to knit. Knit across row.

05. Repeat steps 4 and 5 until throw measures 56 inches from the cast-on edge.

Continued

Weaving in loose ends, *page 113*

Yarn double, *page 129*

FINISHED DIMENSIONS

approximately 46 inches wide
by 56 inches long

06. Bind off. Weave in and trim loose ends.

07. Add fringe. Cut 14-inch pieces of yarn, hold 3 together, and fold in half. Thread through edges of throw at 1-inch intervals. *(You may want to use a crochet hook to help poke the yarn through.)* Trim ends if necessary.

IMPROVISATION IDEA

If you do not want to add fringe and you don't want an end curl, work the first and last 2 inches in garter stitch *(see page 115)*.

YARN CREDIT

Brown Sheep Company "Lamb's Pride Bulky," 85% wool, 15% mohair, 4-ounce skein *(125 yards)*. **Color:** #M-59 Periwinkle, #M-56 Clematis

pillow cover button-up

This comfy pillow with a low-key pattern is the perfect addition to any couch. It also makes a great housewarming gift. Knitting down (on smaller needles than called for on the yarn label) makes a firm yet still pliable rib. The "wrong side" of this stitch pattern is nice too, as it forms a nubby pattern that's visually and texturally interesting.

01. Cast on 53 stitches, leaving a 6-inch tail of yarn to weave in later.

02. Row 1: Knit. *(This is the right side of the piece.)*

03. Row 2: Knit 1, * purl 1, knit 1. Repeat from * to end of row.

04. Repeat steps 2 and 3 for stitch pattern until pillow cover measures 47 inches from the cast-on edge. End with step 3.

05. Create the 4 buttonholes: Knit across row, binding off stitches 6, 7, 20, 21, 34, 35, 47, and 48. Knit to end. If you like, you can place a stitch marker at each bound-off buttonhole as you go along to make them easier to locate in the next step.

06. Next row: Work in stitch pattern *(step 3)*, casting on 2 stitches at each of the 4 bound-off locations.

07. Continue in stitch pattern for 1½ more inches, ending with step 3.

08. Bind off purlwise on the knit row *(step 2)*.

09. Fold pillow cover in half with right sides facing in and the cast-on and bound-off edges aligned. Use your yarn needle to seam the 2 sides.

GAUGE

should be about 3 stitches per inch in stitch pattern on size 9 needles. Adjust needle size if necessary to obtain correct gauge.

YOU WILL NEED

10 skeins (50 grams each) bulky wool

18-inch-by-18-inch pillow form

1 pair size 9 needles, straight or circular (you will work flat, but it's easier to fit all of the stitches onto a circular needle)

4 stitch markers (optional)

Tape measure

Scissors

Yarn needle

Four 1½-inch buttons

Sewing thread to match buttons

Sewing needle

Extra polyester fiber (optional)

TECHNIQUES

Binding off, *page 112*

Casting on, *page 108*

Continued

10. Weave in and trim loose ends.

11. Turn pillow cover right side out, and place pillow form inside. You may want to stuff a little bit of polyester fiber in the corners to plump them out.

12. Sew buttons to wrong side of pillow, corresponding to the 4 buttonholes.

13. Button the pillow up.

IMPROVISATION IDEA

If you don't want the buttons to take such a leading role, you can fold the cover so that the buttons are aligned across the pillow back, 4 inches below the top edge. Leave a 5½-inch flap at the pillow top to fold over and button down. Seam accordingly.

YARN CREDIT

Debbie Bliss "Merino Chunky," 100% merino wool, 50-gram ball *(50 meters).*
Color: #140505

Making seams, *page 120*

Weaving in loose ends, *page 113*

FINISHED DIMENSIONS

approximately 18 inches wide by 49 inches long, assembled to 18 inches square plus button flap should be about 2¾ stitches per inch in stockinette stitch on a size 10 needle. Adjust needle size if necessary to obtain correct gauge.

YOU WILL NEED

1 skein (3 ounces) bulky acrylic or washable wool (makes 1 hat and 2 pairs of booties)

1 size 9 circular needle, 16 inches long (to work flat)

1 pair size 10 needles, straight or circular

2 size 9 double-pointed needles (for I-cord ties)

Tape measure

Scissors

Yarn needle

2 small stitch holders

TECHNIQUES

Binding off, *page 112*

Casting on, *page 108*

Garter stitch, *page 115*

baby shower set ^{lickety-split}

If you want to gift something handmade for a little one but don't have enough time to do something very involved, this is the project for you. It only takes a few hours, and baby will look like an adorable little elf in the peaked cap. If you have a whole weekend, you might want to do a blanket in matching yarn.

HAT

01. Cast 32 stitches on your size 9 circular needle, leaving a 6-inch tail to weave in later.

02. Work 1 inch in knit 1, purl 1 ribbing. Change to size 10 needles.

03. Knit 1 row.

04. Purl 1 row.

05. Knit 2 rows. *(The second knit row creates the garter stitch ridge.)*

06. Repeat steps 3 through 5 until hat measures 5¾ inches from cast-on edge.

07. Working in pattern, bind off the first 4 stitches of each row until no stitches remain.

08. Fold hat with wrong side facing out, and seam from top to bottom. A peak will form at the top.

09. Using your size 9 circular needle, pick up and knit 28 stitches around the base of the hat.

10. Work 1 inch in knit 1, purl 1 ribbing.

Continued

Joining a new strand of yarn
(booties only), *page 114*

Making I-cord, *page 32*

Making seams, *page 120*

Picking up stitches (booties
only), *page 122*

Rib stitch, *page 115*

Stockinette stitch, *page 115*

Weaving in loose ends, *page 113*

FINISHED DIMENSIONS

Hat: approximately 6 inches
high and 6½ inches wide at top
(13 inches wide, unseamed)

Booties: approximately 3½
inches tall (with tops unrolled)
and 4 inches long from toe
to heel

11. Bind off in pattern.

12. Create 2 skinny I-cord ties: Cast 2 stitches on a size 9 double-pointed
needle. Knit 1 row. Slide stitches to opposite end of needle, bringing yarn
around the back to knit next row. Continue until tie measures 8 inches
long. Bind off. Sew to the bottom corners of the neck ribbing, as pictured.
Repeat to make a second tie.

13. Weave in and trim loose ends.

BOOTIES (MAKE 2 OR 4)

Cast 16 stitches on your size 9 circular needle, leaving a 6-inch tail to weave
in later.

Work 1 inch in knit 1, purl 1 ribbing.

Change to size 10 needles.

Knit 1 row.

Purl 1 row.

Knit 2 rows.

Repeat steps 4 through 6.

Divide for instep: Knit 5, then place these stitches on a small stitch holder.
Knit 6. Slide the remaining 5 stitches off the needle and onto a second
stitch holder.

Working with the 6 active stitches, continue in pattern for 1½ inches.
(You are at the purl row part of the stitch pattern right now.) Cut yarn.

Now you will knit around the entire bootie. Slide 5 stitches from the first
holder onto a needle. Pick up 4 stitches from the side of the foot with the

same needle. Slide the 6 active stitches onto the needle. Continue around the other side of the foot, picking up 4 stitches from the other side. Slide the remaining 5 stitches from the second holder onto the needle—24 stitches total. Don't worry—the toe will pucker a bit.

Join yarn. Work 1½ inches in garter stitch *(knit all stitches, every row)*. Bind off.

Fold the bootie in half with the wrong side out and seam the sole. Seam the back from top to bottom.

Weave in and trim loose ends.

Repeat steps to make second bootie.

IMPROVISATION IDEA

If you want to enlarge the hat to fit a one-year-old, cast on 40 stitches and work for 6¾ inches.

YARN CREDIT

Lion Brand "Jiffy," 100% acrylic, 3-ounce skein *(135 yards)*.
Color: #158 Lemon

dog sweater

Dogs come in so many shapes and sizes that it's hard to write a pattern to fit all. You can just work the pattern as is, based on weight, or you can measure your dog from the base of the neck to the tail and adjust the length accordingly. Because of the button-up straps under the dog's belly and around the neck, you can fiddle with button placement or quickly unknit a bit if these straps seem too loose. This pattern fits a miniature (10 pounds and under) dog with sizes for small (11–24 pounds) and medium (25–40 pounds) in parentheses.

01. Cast 12 *(16, 20)* stitches on your needle, leaving a 6-inch tail to weave in later.

02. Work 2 rows in garter stitch *(knit all stitches, every row)*.

03. Increase row *(right side)*: Knit 2, increase 1, knit until 3 stitches remain, increase 1, knit 2—2 stitches increased.

04. Knit 2, purl until 2 stitches remain, knit 2.

05. Repeat steps 3 and 4 for stitch pattern, keeping the first and last 2 stitches in garter stitch, the stitches between in stockinette stitch, until there are 26 *(34, 40)* stitches on your needle. Work increased stitches in stockinette stitch.

Continued

FINISHED DIMENSIONS

approximately 12 (15, 18) inches
wide, 10½ (15, 18) inches from
base to neck. Neck flaps are 3½
(5½, 7½) inches long and 3 (4,
4½) inches wide. Belly strap is
3 (3½, 4) inches wide and 5 (7,
9) inches long.

06. Work even in stitch pattern until sweater measures 10½ *(15, 19½)* inches
from the cast-on edge. End with a wrong-side row *(step 4)*.

07. Shape neck *(right side)*: Knit 10 *(13, 15)* stitches. Join a second ball of yarn,
and bind off 6 *(8, 10)* center stitches. Work to end—10 *(13, 15)* stitches
each side.

08. Working both sides at the same time, at each neck edge, bind off 2 *(3, 3)*
stitches every other row 1 time—8 *(10, 12)* stitches remain for each shoulder.
Work 1 row even.

09. Next row: Bind off 1 *(1, 2)* stitch at each neck edge—7 *(9, 10)* stitches remain
for each shoulder. Work 1 row even.

10. Create garter stitch border: Keeping the first and last 2 stitches in garter
stitch and the stitches between in stockinette stitch, work until neck flaps
measure 3 *(5, 7)* inches from first neck bind-off row.

11. Work 3 rows in garter stitch. Bind off.

12. Create the collar: Pick up and knit 12 *(16, 20)* stitches around neck, in the
U-shaped area between the garter-stitch-edged section.

13. Work 3 *(4, 4)* rows in knit 1, purl 1 ribbing. Bind off in pattern.

14. Create underbelly strap: Cast on 8 *(10, 12)* stitches. Work in knit 1, purl 1
ribbing for 5 *(7, 9)* inches. Bind off in pattern.

15. Center strap at midpoint between the base of the neck and the end of the
sweater, and use your yarn needle to sew 1 side to sweater. Sew 2 buttons
at midpoint on the opposite side of the sweater with sewing needle and
thread. You will be able to secure the buttons without buttonholes, as the
weave of the chunky yarn is so loose.

16. Sew 2 buttons to the garter stitch edging on the neck flap at 1 side of the collar. Again, you will be able to secure the buttons without buttonholes.

17. Weave in and trim loose ends.

IMPROVISATION IDEA

You can create a more turtleneck-like effect if you add a few extra inches in step 13.

YARN CREDIT

Filatura Di Crosa "ZarOne," 50% wool, 50% acrylic, 50-gram ball *(55 meters)*.
Color: #538

cat mat

Here's an afghan for the most important member of your household. Put it in a closet where Princess likes to sleep, so she doesn't fur up your clothes, or put it under a chair where she likes to be, so she doesn't fur up the rug. It's also great for those dreaded cat carrier moments.

01. Cast on 55 stitches, leaving a 6-inch tail to weave in later.

02. Work 3 inches in garter stitch *(knit all stitches, every row).*

03. Place markers for border and central ridge: Knit 7 stitches, place marker, purl 20 stitches, place marker, knit 1 stitch, place marker, purl 20 stitches, place marker, knit remaining 7 stitches.

04. Knit across next row. *(This is the right side of the piece.)*

05. Knit 7, slip marker, purl 20, slip marker, knit 1, slip marker, purl 20, slip marker, end knit 7.

06. Repeat steps 4 and 5.

07. Next row: Work a right-side row as in step 5, creating a garter stitch ridge.

08. Repeat step 5, then repeat steps 4 and 5 two times for 5 rows total, ending with step 5.

09. Repeat steps 7 and 8 for stitch pattern until mat measures 20 inches from the cast-on edge. End by working a knit row after the last repeat of step 5.

GAUGE

should be about 2 stitches per inch in stockinette stitch on a size 13 needle. Adjust needle size if necessary to obtain correct gauge.

YOU WILL NEED

3 skeins (6 ounces each) bulky washable wool or acrylic

1 size 13 circular needle, 29 inches long

4 stitch markers

Tape measure

Scissors

Yarn needle

TECHNIQUES

Binding off, *page 112*

Casting on, *page 108*

Garter stitch, *page 115*

Stockinette stitch, *page 115*

Weaving in loose ends, *page 113*

Continued

FINISHED DIMENSIONS

approximately 30 inches wide
by 23 inches long

10. Knit 3 inches in garter stitch.

11. Bind off. Cut yarn, and weave in and trim loose ends.

IMPROVISATION IDEA

Double the dimensions to make
a mat that's perfect for a medium
to large dog.

YARN CREDIT

Lion Brand "Wool-Ease Thick +
Quick," 80% acrylic, 20% wool,
6-ounce ball (108 yards).
Color: #182 Pine

tank top ^{toddler}

Here's a basic tank to keep your little one cool and stylish this summer. Work it all in one color, or do the simple crochet slip stitch edging in an accent color as pictured. This pattern fits an eighteen- to twenty-four-month-old. Directions to fit a two-year-old and a three-year-old are given in parentheses. Don't forget the sunscreen!

01. Cast 26 *(28, 30)* stitches on a size 10½ needle, leaving a 6-inch tail to weave in later.

02. Row 1: Purl *(right side)*.

03. Row 2: Purl *(wrong side)*.

04. Row 3: Knit.

05. Continue working in stockinette stitch *(repeating steps 3 and 4)*, until top measures 7 *(7½, 8½)* inches. End with a wrong-side *(purl)* row *(step 3)*.

06. Shape armholes: Bind off 2 stitches at the beginning of the next 2 rows—4 stitches total bound off; 22 *(24, 26)* stitches total remain.

07. Bind off 1 stitch at the beginning of the next 4 *(4, 6)* rows—18 *(20, 20)* stitches total remain.

08. Work even until piece measures 10 *(10½, 11½)* inches from the cast-on edge, ending with a wrong-side row.

Continued

GAUGE

should be about 2¾ stitches per inch in stockinette stitch on size 10½ needles. Adjust needle size if necessary to obtain correct gauge.

YOU WILL NEED

2 skeins (50 grams each) bulky cotton or cotton-blend yarn

1 pair size 10½ needles

1 size 10½ crochet hook

Tape measure

Scissors

Yarn needle

TECHNIQUES

Binding off, *page 112*

Casting on, *page 108*

Crocheting slip stitch, *page 125*

Decreasing, *page 117*

Joining a new strand of yarn, *page 114*

Making seams, *page 120*

Stockinette stitch, *page 115*

Weaving in loose ends, *page 113*

09. Next row, shape neck: Work 6 *(7, 7)* stitches; join a second ball of yarn and bind off 6 *(6, 6)* center stitches. Work to end—6 *(7, 7)* stitches each shoulder.

10. Working both sides at the same time, at each neck edge, decrease 1 stitch every other row 1 *(2, 2)* time—2 *(4, 4)* stitches total bound off; 1 *(2, 2)* stitch per side. 5 *(5, 5)* stitches remain for each shoulder.

11. Work even on remaining 5 stitches until each side measures 12¼ *(13, 14¼)* inches from cast-on edge to top of shoulder strap, ending with a wrong-side row. Bind off.

12. Repeat steps 1 through 11 to make back.

13. Finishing: Place the 2 pieces together with wrong sides facing out. Using your yarn needle, seam shoulders, then sides. Weave in and trim loose ends.

14. Use your crochet hook and a strand of the same type of yarn *(the color is your choice)* to edge the neck and armholes in slip stitch. Secure yarn and trim.

IMPROVISATION IDEA

Alternate colors every 2 rows to make a cheery, striped tank. You could also knit this in wool and use it over a turtleneck as a winter vest.

YARN CREDIT

Lana Grossa "Soft Cotton," 60% cotton, 40% microfiber, 50-gram ball *(75 meters)*.
Colors: #022, #2 *(edging)*

FINISHED DIMENSIONS

approximately 9½ (10, 10¾) inches wide for body, 7 (7½, 8½) inches to armhole, 12¼ (13, 14¼) inches to shoulder. Shoulders are 2½ inches wide for all sizes. Neck is 3 (3¾, 3¾) inches wide.

should be about 3 stitches per inch in stitch pattern on a size 9 needle. Adjust needle size if necessary to obtain correct gauge. Exact gauge is not critical for this project.

YOU WILL NEED

5 skeins (3½ ounces each) bulky superwash wool

1 size 9 circular needle, 29 inches long

2 stitch markers

Tape measure

Scissors

Yarn needle

Row counter

TECHNIQUES

Binding off, *page 112*

Casting on, *page 108*

Garter stitch, *page 115*

Weaving in loose ends, *page 113*

Zigzag stitch

zigzag baby blanket

Festive zigzags dance across the surface of this cuddly baby blanket. This is one of the more time-consuming projects in the book, but the beautiful result is well worth the time spent! Use a row counter to keep track of where you are.

01. Cast on 80 stitches, leaving a 6-inch tail to weave in later.

02. Knit 8 stitches, place marker. Knit until 8 stitches remain, place second marker. Knit remaining 8 stitches.

03. Work 2½ inches in garter stitch *(knit all stitches, every row)*, slipping markers as you go.

04. Row 1 *(right side)*: Knit 8, slip marker. Knit 7, * purl 2, knit 6. Repeat from *, ending last repeat with knit 7. Slip marker, knit 8.

05. Row 2: Knit 8, slip marker. Knit 2, * purl 4, knit 4. Repeat from *, ending with knit 2. Slip marker, knit 8.

06. Row 3: Knit 8, slip marker. Knit 1, * purl 2, knit 2. Repeat from *, ending with knit 1. Slip marker, knit 8.

07. Row 4: Knit 8, slip marker. Knit 1, purl 1, * knit 4, purl 4. Repeat from *, ending with knit 4, purl 1, knit 1. Slip marker, knit 8.

08. Row 5: Knit 8, slip marker. Knit 3, * purl 2, knit 6. Repeat from *, ending with knit 3. Slip marker, knit 8.

09. Row 6: Knit 8, slip marker. Knit 1, * purl 6, knit 2. Repeat from *, ending with knit 1. Slip marker, knit 8.

Continued

FINISHED DIMENSIONS

approximately 26 inches wide by
31 inches long

10. Row 7: Knit 8, slip marker. Knit 1, purl 1, * knit 4, purl 4. Repeat from *, ending with knit 4, purl 1, knit 1. Slip marker, knit 8.

11. Row 8: Knit 8, slip marker. Knit 3, * purl 2, knit 2. Repeat from *, ending with knit 3. Slip marker, knit 8.

12. Row 9: Knit 8, slip marker. Knit 2, * purl 4, knit 4. Repeat from *, ending with knit 2. Slip marker, knit 8.

13. Row 10: Knit 8, slip marker. Knit 1, purl 2, * knit 2, purl 6. Repeat from * until 5 stitches remain before second marker. Knit 2, purl 2, knit 1. Slip marker, knit 8.

14. Repeat steps 4 through 13 until blanket measures approximately 28½ inches from cast-on edge.

15. Work 2½ inches in garter stitch, removing markers as you come to them on the first row.

16. Bind off. Cut yarn. Using your yarn needle, weave in and trim loose ends.

IMPROVISATION IDEA

If you want to make the blanket faster, get some chunkier yarn, figure out what the gauge is, then adapt the pattern stitch in multiples of 8 stitches.

YARN CREDIT

Brown Sheep Company "Lamb's Pride Superwash Bulky," 100% wool, 3½-ounce skein (110 yards).
Color: Blaze

tank dress toddler

Here's a cool tank dress, classy enough for summer parties, comfy enough for serious playground romps. If you like, you can edge the armholes and neck with a simple crochet slip stitch. This pattern fits an average-size eighteen-month-old. Directions to fit a two-year-old, three-year-old, and four-year-old are in parentheses.

01. Cast 88 *(96, 104, 112)* stitches on your needle, leaving a 6-inch tail to weave in later.

02. Place marker and join, being careful not to twist the stitches. Knit 1 round, placing a second marker halfway, after 44 *(48, 52, 56)* stitches.

03. Round 2: Purl *(for edging)*.

04. Rounds 3 and 4: Knit.

05. Round 5: Purl.

06. You will work in stockinette stitch for the rest of the dress. Knit 0 *(2, 2, 4)* rounds even.

07. Decrease round: Round 6 *(8, 8, 10)*: Slip first marker, slip 1, knit 1, pass slipped stitch over. Knit to 2 stitches before second marker, knit 2 together. Slip second marker, slip 1, knit 1, pass slipped stitch over. Knit to 2 stitches before first marker, knit 2 together—4 stitches decreased.

08. Continue working in stockinette stitch, repeating decrease round every 8 *(8, 8, 7)* rounds, 5 *(6, 7, 8)* times total—20 *(24, 28, 32)* stitches total decreased; 68 *(72, 76, 80)* stitches remain.

09. Work even until dress measures 11¾ *(13, 14¼, 15½)* inches from the cast-on edge.

GAUGE

should be about 3 stitches per inch and 4 rows per inch in stockinette stitch on a size 10 needle. Adjust needle size if necessary to obtain correct gauge.

YOU WILL NEED

4 (4, 5, 5) skeins (50 grams each) bulky cotton or cotton-blend yarn

1 size 10 circular needle, 24 inches long

1 size 10 crochet hook (optional)

2 stitch markers

Tape measure

Scissors

Yarn needle

Row counter

Large stitch holder

TECHNIQUES

Binding off, *page 112*

Casting on, *page 108*

Crocheting slip stitch (optional), *page 125*

Decreasing, *page 117*

Garter stitch, *page 115*

Joining a new strand of yarn, *page 114*

Knitting in the round, *page 119*

Making seams, *page 120*

Stockinette stitch, *page 115*

Weaving in loose ends, *page 113*

FINISHED DIMENSIONS

approximately 15 (16, 17, 18) inches wide at bottom of dress, 15¾ (18, 20¼, 22½) inches long from bottom of dress to top of shoulder. Shoulder strap is 2 inches wide for all sizes. Neck is 3½ (4, 4½, 5¼) inches wide.

10. Divide for armholes: Place half of the stitches on your large stitch holder. You will be working the front and back separately, on 34 *(36, 38, 40)* stitches.

11. Bind off 3 stitches at the beginning of the next 2 rows.

12. Bind off 2 stitches at the beginning of the next 2 rows.

13. Bind off 1 stitch at the beginning of the next 2 rows—12 stitches total decreased; 22 *(24, 26, 28)* stitches remain.

14. Work even until dress measures 14¼ *(16½, 18¾, 21)* inches, ending with a wrong-side row.

15. Shape neck *(right side)*: Work 8 *(8, 8, 8)* stitches; join a second ball of yarn and bind off center 6 *(8, 10, 12)* stitches; work to end—8 *(8, 8, 8)* stitches each shoulder.

16. Working both sides at the same time, at each neck edge, bind off 2 stitches every other row once—a total of 10 *(12, 14, 16)* neck stitches bound off; 6 stitches remain on each side for shoulder straps.

17. Shoulder straps: Work even on remaining 12 stitches *(6 stitches per shoulder)*, until dress measures 15¾ *(18, 20¼, 22½)* inches, ending with a wrong-side row. Bind off.

18. Place stitches from large holder on needle. Repeat steps 11 through 17 for back.

19. Seam shoulders. Use crochet hook to edge the neck and armholes in slip stitch (optional). Weave in and trim loose ends.

IMPROVISATION IDEA

If you want a neck that's scoopier, start shaping it about 2½ inches from the end length.

YARN CREDIT

Rowan "Cotton Rope," 55% cotton, 45% acrylic, 50-gram ball *(58 meters)*.
Color: #061

techniques

This chapter includes instructions for the techniques you'll need to know to complete the projects in this book. You'll learn how to cast on and bind off, knit and purl, increase, decrease, and yarn over. It explains the difference between knitting on two needles and knitting in the round.

holding the
needles

The first step in learning to knit is deciding how to hold the needles. There are a few variations; experiment until you find the way that feels most comfortable. The directions below are for both left- and right-handed knitters.

LEFT HAND

The needle holding the stitches rests in your left hand. The stitch nearest the end should be about 1 inch from the needle's tip. Hold the needle with your index finger at the first stitch. Or, if you're knitting Continental style, hold the needle with your middle finger at the first stitch (*see page 110*). Your thumb rests on the opposite side of the needle to stabilize it. The remaining three fingers curl under to balance the needle.

RIGHT HAND

Rest your index finger on the top of the needle, about 2 inches from the tip. Place your thumb about an inch lower, on the opposite side. Lightly curl the remaining three fingers lower around the needle.

positioning the
yarn

The two most common methods of knitting are American and Continental. In the American style, you hold and move the yarn with your right hand. In the Continental style, you hold and move the yarn with your left hand. Try both to see which you feel more comfortable with. Eventually you will want to know both styles, as it's helpful for Fair Isle knitting, in which you work with two colors of yarn at a time.

AMERICAN STYLE

The ball of yarn should be to your right. Rest the strand that leads from your left needle to the ball on top of your right index finger, then wrap it under your middle finger, over your third finger, and let the rest trail down to your ball under the little finger *(FIGURE 1A)*.

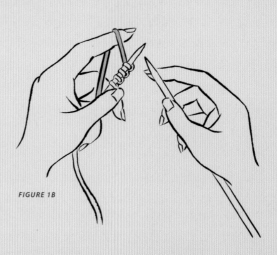

FIGURE 1B

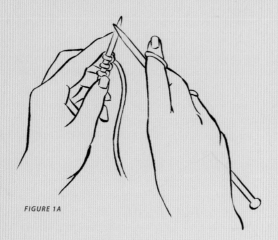

FIGURE 1A

CONTINENTAL STYLE

Place the ball of yarn to your left and weave the yarn that leads from your left needle to the ball over your left index finger, under the middle finger, over the third finger, and let it trail down to the ball under the little finger *(FIGURE 1B)*. If you are left-handed, you may find this method easier.

There are many other ways to hold the yarn. It needs to be neither too loose nor too tight as you work with it. Some people like to wrap the yarn loosely around a finger to help maintain the correct tension. Experiment and do what works best for you.

casting on

All knitting begins with a cast-on row. The number of cast-on stitches determines the size of the piece you are knitting. There are several ways to cast on. The instructions here offer the method known as knit cast-on, which uses two needles. Practice with a pair of size 8 or 9 single-point, 10-inch needles and some acrylic yarn. Place the ball of yarn to your right and pull out a few feet of yarn.

1. Form a slipknot 8 inches from the end of the yarn. To do this, make a small loop of yarn. Pinch a second loop of yarn from the yarn end, about an inch below the first loop, pull it around and thread it

FIGURE 2

FIGURE 3A

FIGURE 3B

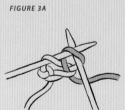

FIGURE 3C

through the backside of the first loop. Grasp the second loop and draw the first loop closed by pulling the yarn end that leads to the ball *(FIGURE 2)*. Slide the slip-knot onto a needle and tighten the knot until it is a little larger in circumference than the needle. Hold the needle with the stitch in your left hand.

2. Taking the second needle in your right hand, thread the yarn that leads to the ball over your right index finger, below your middle finger, and over your third finger, letting the rest fall beneath your little finger down toward the ball *(SEE FIGURE 1A, PAGE 107)*.

3. Insert your right needle through the front of the stitch on your left needle, forming an X with your needles *(FIGURE 3A)*. Raise your right index finger and loop yarn from the ball end around the right needle from back to front. Dip and pull the right needle toward you, away from the left needle, catching the newly formed loop *(FIGURE 3B)*.

4. Slip the new loop on the right needle onto your left needle *(FIGURE 3C)*. You now have two cast-on stitches on the left needle. Repeat until you have 20 or so stitches. You may want to practice casting on a few times before moving on to learning the knit stitch.

american style

Make sure that your cast-on row is not twisted and that the bottoms *(the chunky part)* of the stitches are aligned and evenly spaced. Hold the needle with the cast-on row in your left hand. Hold the yarn American style, as directed in "Positioning the Yarn" *(page 107)*, letting the rest fall beneath your little finger down toward the ball.

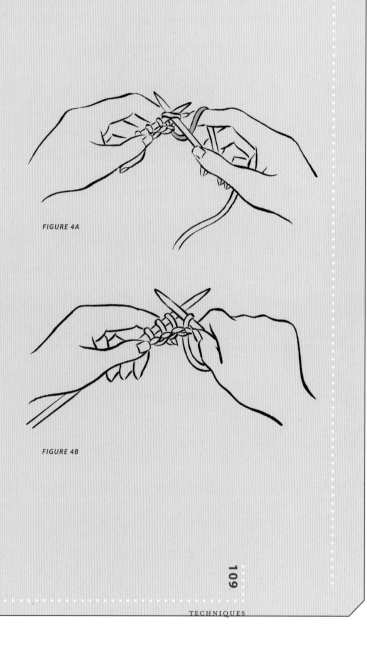

FIGURE 4A

1. Insert your right needle through the first stitch on the left needle forming an **X** with your needles *(FIGURE 4A)*.

2. Raise your right index finger and loop the yarn around the right needle from back to front. Dip and pull the right needle toward you, away from the left needle, catching the newly formed loop.

3. Leaving the new loop on your right needle, pull the right needle with the new stitch toward you, away from the left needle, and let the rest of the original stitch slip off the left needle. This is your first knit stitch *(FIGURE 4B)*.

4. Repeat until you reach the end of the row. At that point, you will shift the right-hand needle *(which is now full of stitches)* back to your left hand.

FIGURE 4B

continental style

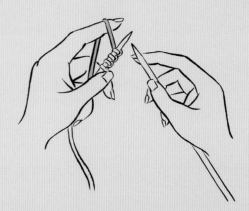

Make sure that your cast-on row is not twisted and that the bottoms *(the chunky part)* of the stitches are aligned and evenly spaced. Hold the needle with the cast-on row in your left hand. Hold the yarn Continental style, as directed in "Positioning the Yarn" *(page 107)*, letting the rest fall beneath your little finger down toward the ball.

1. Insert your right needle through the first stitch on the left needle, forming an **X** with your needles.

2. Raise your left index finger and loop the yarn around the right needle, wrapping it from left to right. Dip and pull the right needle toward you, away from the left needle, catching the newly formed loop.

3. Leaving the new loop on your right needle, pull the right needle with the new stitch toward you, away from the left needle, and let the rest of the original stitch slip off the left needle. This is your first knit stitch.

4. Repeat until you reach the end of the row. At that point, you will shift the right-hand needle *(which is now full of stitches)* back to your left hand.

You may find it helpful to remember the steps of the knit stitch with a traditional poem that has been handed down for generations:

> *In through the front door,*
>
> *Once around the back,*
>
> *Peek through the window,*
>
> *And off jumps Jack.*

Practice the knit stitch until you feel comfortable, and then move on to the purl stitch. You can make the Classic Skinny Scarf *(page 18)* using the knit stitch, casting on, and binding off. If you have never knit before, you may want to try this project first.

the
purl stitch

When you made the knit stitch, you worked with the yarn held behind the left needle. When you make the purl stitch, you will be working with the yarn held **in front** of the left needle. Knit and purl are the two basic stitches that make up almost every other type of stitch in knitting, so once you learn them both you will be well on your way to becoming a master. Hold the needles and the yarn the same way you did for the knit stitch, either American or Continental style. The only difference is that you hold the yarn that leads to the ball **in front** of the left needle. If you hold it behind the needle, it will be impossible to catch it in the right way to form a purl stitch.

1. Insert your right needle through the first stitch on the left needle *(FIGURE 5A)*.

2. Raise your right index finger *(or your left index finger, if you are knitting in the Continental style)*, and loop the yarn from the ball end around the right needle from back to front *(FIGURE 5B)*.

3. Dip and pull the right needle away from you, catching the newly formed loop *(FIGURE 5C)*. Leaving the new loop on your right needle, pull the right needle with the new stitch away from you, and away from the left needle. Let the rest of the original stitch slip off the left needle. This is your first purl stitch *(FIGURE 5D)*.

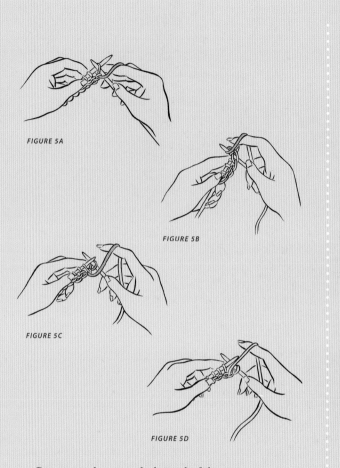

FIGURE 5A

FIGURE 5B

FIGURE 5C

FIGURE 5D

5. Repeat until you reach the end of the row. At that point, you will shift the right-hand needle *(which is now full of stitches)* back to your left hand.

111

binding off

So you've knit a good, long strip and you want to get it off the needles and secure it so it doesn't unravel. This process is called binding off.

1. Start at the beginning of a row and knit 2 stitches in the usual way. You now have 2 stitches on your right needle.

2. Insert your left needle into the front of the first stitch on your right needle *(FIGURE 6A)*.

3. Pull the first stitch over the top of the second stitch and off the needle *(FIGURES 6B AND 6C)*. You now have 1 stitch on your right needle.

4. Knit one more stitch. Again, you have 2 stitches on your right needle. Repeat steps 2 and 3. Continue in this manner until 1 stitch remains on your right needle and none remain on your left. At this point cut the yarn *(leaving about a 6-inch tail to weave in later)* and draw the end of the yarn through the center of the final stitch. Pull to tighten it into a knot.

You can also bind off on a purl row. All you have to do is repeat the sequence above with purl stitches instead of knit stitches.

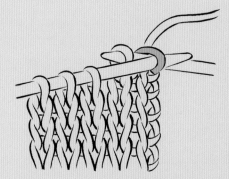

FIGURE 6A

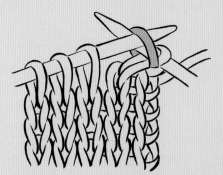

FIGURE 6B

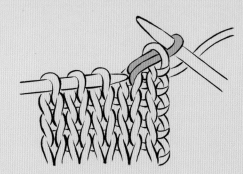

FIGURE 6C

weaving in
loose ends

You will be faced with many loose ends of yarn over the course of your knitting career—when you cast on, bind off, sew pieces together, or add a new color or an extra ball of yarn. All you need to do to hide these ends is to thread them, one by one, onto a yarn needle and weave the yarn into the edges or the wrong side of your knitting. When you feel the yarn end is secure *(usually after about 3 inches)*, remove the needle and trim the yarn.

picking up
dropped stitches

Even if you are very careful, you will eventually drop a stitch. While it's annoying, it's no reason to throw in the towel. Simply fix it with your trusty crochet hook. The dropped stitch will unravel downward into the fabric you've already knit, creating a ladder *(FIGURE 7)*. Here's what to do.

1. Push the remaining stitches toward the knob end of your needle so they won't fall off. If you were working on a purl row *(if the wrong side of the piece is facing you; see page 115)*, turn the work around so the knit stitches are facing you.

2. Catch the top of the dropped loop with your crochet hook.

3. Slide the loop down below the hook, and use the hook itself to latch onto the rung of the ladder directly above the dropped stitch. Pull the rung through the loop, being careful not to twist it.

4. Use the hook to catch the next strand of the ladder. Keep going until you reach the needle, placing the last loop back where it belongs, on either your right or left knitting needle.

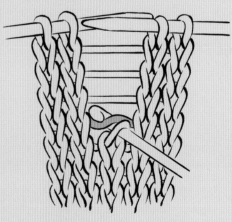

FIGURE 7

new strand of yarn

When your yarn ball runs out before your piece is finished, you'll need to join a new strand of yarn. There are many ways to do this. I prefer to tie the new piece in *(method 1)*, but everyone has a favorite method. Here are a few to choose from.

METHOD 1.

Join a new strand by tying the new strand around the old in a slipknot. This should be done at the beginning of a row. Slide the knot up as close as possible to the knit fabric, and just start knitting with the new ball. Later you will weave the loose ends into the knit piece.

METHOD 2.

If you are joining the same color of yarn, you can simply knit with both the new yarn and the old one for 2 or 3 stitches to secure it, and then continue on with new yarn alone. Again, you will go back later and weave the loose ends into the knit fabric. You may be afraid that the double-strand part will be lumpy, but it blends in nicely with the rest of the fabric.

METHOD 3.

If you must join yarn in the middle of a row, you may want to meld the new and old yarns together. Thread a yarn needle with the new yarn and weave it into the end of the old yarn for about 3 inches. Remove the needle and give the yarn a little pull to secure it and straighten it out. Leave the short tail on the wrong side of the knit piece *(see page 115)*, and trim it off later.

METHOD 4.

Occasionally, as when you start the thumb of a mitten or work around a baby bootie, you will have to join new yarn to nothing but a row of stitches. In this case, anchor the loose end of the new ball with your hand to prevent the yarn from slipping. It may feel awkward, but after the first few stitches it will secure.

creating patterns with
stitches

You've learned the two basic stitches you will use over and over again—the knit stitch and the purl stitch. But there are many ways to combine these stitches to create very different patterns and textures. Here are just a few.

GARTER STITCH

This basic stitch is created simply by knitting every row. The knitted fabric looks the same on both sides with a series of ridges and does not curl at the edges. This is the easiest stitch.

STOCKINETTE STITCH

In the stockinette stitch, you knit one row and purl the next. Most store-bought sweaters are knit predominantly in stockinette stitch. The knitted fabric has a smooth side that looks like it is formed of tiny V's and a bumpier side.

Many patterns refer to the knit side of stockinette as the "right" side and to the purl side as the "wrong" side.

RIB STITCH

Ribbing is created when the knit and purl stitches alternate in a row. Ribbing is often seen on items that require snug, non-curling edges, such as sweaters and mittens. To make a knit 1, purl 1 ribbing, cast on an even number of stitches. Work across the row, knitting 1 stitch and purling the next. You'll need to move the yarn from back to front and vice versa in order to alternate stitches. When you reach the end of the row, repeat the same pattern of stitches for the next row. To make a knit 2, purl 2 ribbing, cast on an even number of stitches in a multiple of 4, as the pattern will repeat every 4 stitches. Work across the row, knitting 2 stitches and then purling 2 stitches. Repeat the same pattern for the next row.

SEED STITCH

This textured stitch, also called a moss stitch, is created by alternating knit and purl stitches from row to row. Cast on an even number of stitches and alternate between the knit and purl stitches as follows:

Row 1: Knit, purl, knit, purl, knit, purl, knit, purl, knit, purl . . .

Row 2: Purl, knit, purl, knit, purl, knit, purl, knit, purl, knit . . .

In other words, after the first row you purl the smooth stitches and knit the bumpy ones.

increasing

Sometimes you'll need to make a piece of knitting wider, such as when you shape the sleeve of a sweater. The easiest way to increase is to turn one stitch into two by knitting or purling it twice.

1. Slide your needle into a stitch as if to knit, and wrap the yarn around the needle as usual. Catch the newly formed loop and pull it away with the right needle. Instead of letting the rest of the original stitch slide off the needle, leave the new loop on the right needle and the rest of the original stitch on the left.

2. Slip the right needle into the back of the original stitch and wrap the yarn around the needle again; then let it slide off onto the right needle (*FIGURE 8*). You now have 2 stitches instead of 1.

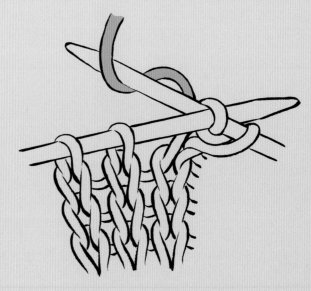

FIGURE 8

decreasing

Sometimes you will need to make a piece of knitting smaller or narrower, such as when you shape the top of a hat. Here are three basic techniques.

1. The easiest way to decrease is to knit or purl 2 stitches together. To do this, simply insert your right needle into two stitches on your left needle and knit or purl them as one, thus creating a single stitch where 2 stitches were previously. This kind of decrease slants to the right.

2. Another way of decreasing is with a technique known as *pass slipped stitch over*. This method is similar to the one described earlier for binding off. This type of decrease will slant to the left. Insert your needle into a stitch as if you were about to knit it. But don't knit it—instead, just slip it off onto the right needle *(FIGURE 9A)*. Knit the next stitch, and then slide the left needle into the front of the slipped stitch on the right needle. Pull the slipped stitch over the stitch in front of it and let it fall off the needle *(FIGURE 9B)*. You now have 1 stitch where you previously had 2.

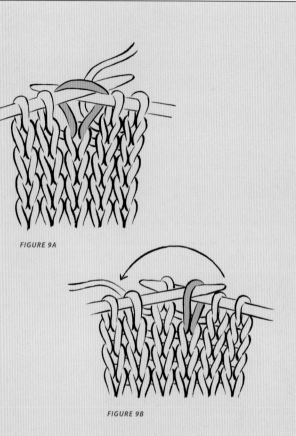

FIGURE 9A

FIGURE 9B

3. The slip, slip, knit decrease slants to the left. Slip 2 stitches to the right needle knitwise, 1 after the other. Place your left needle tip through the front of the slipped stitches. Use your right needle to knit the stitches together through the back of the loops. One stitch remains.

yarn over

The yarn over technique creates the open, lacy look often seen in shawls. This technique increases the number of stitches on your needle and can be done on the knit or purl side.

To do a yarn over on the knit side, wrap the yarn over and around the right needle, from front to back *(FIGURE 10A)*, and then knit the next stitch *(or knit 2 stitches together if directed to do so)*. When you work across the next row, you will see that an open space has been formed.

To do a yarn over on the purl side, bring the yarn from the front of the right needle over the top and around the back *(FIGURE 10B)*, and then purl the next stitch.

fringe

Adding fringe to scarves or shawls adds extra flair, and it's easy to do. First, cut a length of yarn that's double your desired length of fringe. Fold the yarn in half and push the looped end of the yarn through one stitch on the edge of the knit item where you want fringe to be. *(You can use your yarn needle or a crochet hook to help with this.)* Draw the cut ends of the yarn through the loop, and then tighten to make a knot. Trim the ends to even them up.

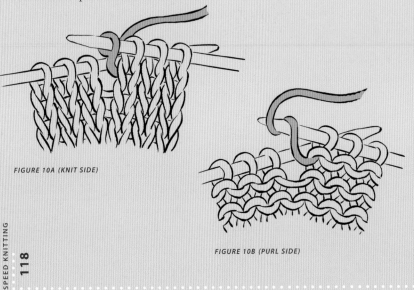

FIGURE 10A (KNIT SIDE)

FIGURE 10B (PURL SIDE)

knitting in
the round

You can make anything—sweaters, hats, mittens—by knitting it in pieces and then sewing it together. But knitting in the round has several advantages that flat knitting doesn't. First, you are creating a stronger, seamless piece. Second, you work faster on circular needles because you knit in a continuous circle rather than flipping the piece over constantly to work a front and a back.

When you knit in the round, you create a circle of stitches and work in "rounds" rather than rows. There are two ways to knit in the round: with circular and with double-pointed needles (*see page 13*). Use a set of four double-pointed needles for smaller projects with tighter rounds, to handle the small number of stitches per needle (*FIGURE 11*). When you are casting on with double-pointed needles, it's easiest to cast all of the stitches required onto one needle and then divide them among the three needles, rather than trying to cast 8 onto one needle, 10 onto another, and 8 more onto a third. Circular needles are great for larger pieces like sweaters and hats, both of which have enough stitches to stretch around a longer cord.

To join a row of stitches into a circle, make sure that your work is not twisted, place a stitch marker (*see page 15*) in front of the

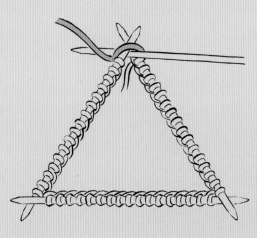

FIGURE 11

first stitch on your right needle(s), and join the first stitch to the last simply by knitting them together. This may seem a little awkward in the beginning, so rest the needles in your lap while you do it. Continue to work in a circle until the desired number of rounds is obtained. Your stitch marker indicates the beginning of the round. One of the beauties of knitting in the round is that you can create the stockinette stitch (*see page 115*) using only the knit stitch: Since you are working in a circle, you never have to turn your work and purl.

making seams

Sewing together pieces of knitting is trickier than sewing pieces of cloth because you're working with a bulkier fabric, and you have to remember to line up stitches and rows. It's always best to pin the pieces together before sewing; otherwise, you will spend a lot of time making sure the ends match up. In addition, you should never make seams too tight.

Knitting is elastic, and your seams should be as well. Experiment with different techniques, and don't hesitate to pull out a few stitches or even an entire seam in order to sew something you're completely satisfied with.

A few of the many different ways to make seams are described on this and the following pages. Whatever method you use, you should always use a yarn needle threaded with about 18 inches of the same type of yarn you used to make your knit fabric. When you make your stitches, be careful not to split the yarn. Instead, pass your needle through the spaces in the stitches.

BACKSTITCH

The backstitch is commonly used to join shoulder, sleeve, and side seams. With this method you will be creating a thin inner seam, so you'll want to stay close to the edge of the fabric while sewing. *(Don't go deeper than 2 stitches in.)*

1. Match the pieces you are sewing together, with wrong sides out. Make sure that your stitches are lined up, and pin the pieces in place.

2. Thread your yarn needle with the same yarn you used to knit the item. Take a stitch through both pieces of fabric, coming up ½ inch away from the corner. Leave about a 6-inch tail of yarn to weave in later.

3. Take a short stitch back to the corner (FIGURE 12A). Secure the yarn by repeating this stitch.

4. Insert the needle again ½ inch in front of the stitch you just made, coming up from the back through to the front of the fabric (FIGURE 12B).

5. Insert the needle in front of the first stitch and sew through to the back, filling in the gap between the stitches.

6. Continue in this manner until you reach the end. Keep the stitches even, and make sure you're not pulling the yarn too tight.

Vary the length of the stitch depending on the fineness of the fabric you are seaming. For instance, you may want to make stitches ¼ inch long when sewing seams in baby clothes and ¾ inch long for seams in bulky sweaters. If seams made with bulky yarn seem too chunky, use the overcast stitch, described next, to join the pieces instead.

FIGURE 12A

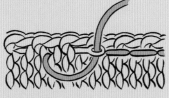

FIGURE 12B

OVERCAST AND MATTRESS STITCHES

The overcast and mattress stitches both make flatter seams than the backstitch. They are great for sewing pillow seams, joining borders or edgings, and joining sections of ribbing. You can also use them to make flatter seams in sweaters.

OVERCAST STITCH

1. Match the pieces you are sewing together, with wrong sides out (*see page 115*) and the stitches lined up. You will be working close to the edge of the fabric, no deeper than the first stitch on each side.

2. Thread your yarn needle with the same yarn you used to knit the item. Starting at the corner, take a stitch through both pieces of fabric, leaving about a 6-inch tail to weave in later. Secure the yarn by inserting the needle back into the same hole, from back to front.

3. Sew through the next matching ridge of fabric, again bringing the thread through from back to front. The yarn will wrap around the edge of the fabric.

4. Continue in this manner until you reach the end of the seam *(FIGURE 13)*. Keep the stitches even, and make sure you're not pulling the yarn too tight.

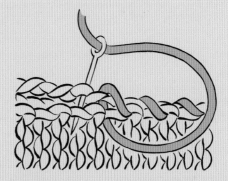

FIGURE 13

MATTRESS STITCH

1. Match the pieces edge to edge, with the stitches lined up and both right sides facing you *(see page 115)*.

2. Thread your yarn needle with the same yarn you used to knit the item. Starting at the left corner and leaving about a 6-inch tail to weave in later, pull the yarn through the middle of the first stitch on the right side.

3. Sew diagonally to the left, coming up in the center of the first stitch in the row above.

4. Repeat, weaving from left to right to left to right, until you reach the end of the section to be joined *(FIGURE 14)*.

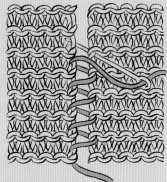

FIGURE 14

Sometimes you will need to pick up stitches from an otherwise finished edge in order to create the collar of a sweater, form the thumb of a mitten, or knit the outer edge of a baby bootie.

To do this, hold the knit item before you so that the outside of the garment is facing you. The edge where the stitches are to be picked up should be at the top. Your pattern will specify how many stitches to pick up, and you will need to space them evenly. To pick up a stitch, insert your knitting needle into the edge of the piece, from front to back, and pull a loop of new yarn through to the front *(FIGURE 15A)*. Continue until you've picked up the number of stitches you need, spacing them evenly across *(FIGURE 15B)*. If the picked-up stitches seem skewed or have a big gap somewhere, take them out and try again.

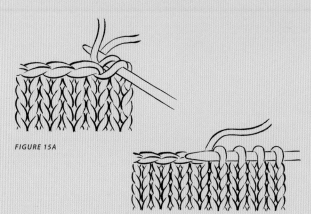

FIGURE 15A

FIGURE 15B

gauge

Gauge refers to the number of stitches per inch and rows per inch. It will change radically depending on the type of yarn you use, the stitch pattern you are knitting, the size of your needles, and how tightly or loosely you tend to knit. *(This can vary, depending on your mood!)* Many patterns specify a gauge to help the knitter more closely achieve the desired results. With that said, gauge is not the be-all and end-all of successful knitting, and for some projects it isn't even an issue. Some of the projects in these pages don't require you to pay much attention to gauge; in most, however, gauge is critical. On larger projects, such as sweaters, more or fewer stitches per inch means the difference between small and large in the finished project.

To determine gauge, you need to knit a small sample, or swatch, of fabric. You must use the specific yarn and needles that you'll be using for the project, and the swatch should be knit in the stitch you will be using. A simple recipe for a 5-inch swatch follows.

1. Check the pattern to see how many stitches per inch it calls for. For example, the gauge may be 4 stitches per inch on size 8 needles. Use size 8 needles to cast on *(see page 108)* at least 20 stitches. Knit in the stitch specified in the project directions until the swatch is at least 5 inches long.

2. Bind off *(see page 112)* and flatten the swatch out beneath your gauge aid, making sure that your stitches are lined up straight both horizontally and vertically and that the stitches at the left and bottom of your swatch window are not partially covered by the gauge aid.

3. Count the number of stitches across. If you knit 4 stitches per inch with this yarn, you can follow the pattern exactly. If you knit more or fewer, you should adjust the number of stitches you cast on or change the needle size. It's *always* easier to adjust your needle size rather than the number of stitches on complicated projects such as sweaters, as one adjustment in the number of stitches leads to many other adjustments.

If you don't have a gauge aid, you can use a steam iron to steam the swatch a bit so it flattens out. *(Don't touch the iron to wool.)* Then pin the swatch flat and use a ruler to measure the stitches per inch and rows per inch.

blocking

Blocking is a finishing technique that smoothes out stitches and coaxes knit pieces into the desired shape. To block your piece, first dampen it with water or steam, then gently shape it on a flat surface and allow it to dry. You do not need to block acrylic pieces, and you should never block ribbing, as it flattens out. Blocking is best for wool, and it gives a professional, finished look to sweaters. Here are a few approaches to blocking.

1. Don't bother. If your pieces are knit smoothly and the stitches are even, you can just ignore this step.

2. After you have sewn together your piece and spread the finished project out to look it over, use a steam iron to dampen it into smoothness. Be careful not to let the iron touch wool. If it does, the wool will burn.

3. Place your knit items flat between two damp towels and let them dry naturally.

4. Dampen the knit item *(it should not be wringing wet)*, shape it, and pin it to a blocking board, using nonrusting pins. Let it dry naturally.

note: Never use blocking to try to stretch or shrink two knit pieces so that they match each other. It doesn't work.

knitting slip stitch

Sometimes a slipped stitch is used for selvage at the end of a row, sometimes it is worked as part of a decrease. It can also be worked to give a ribbed effect. When a pattern tells you to "slip one" or to "slip a stitch" do the following:

1. Insert your right-hand needle into the next stitch on your left-hand needle as if to knit *(FIGURE 16A)*. *(The instructions will read "as if to purl" if this is required.)*

2. Slip the stitch from your left-hand needle to the right-hand needle without knitting or purling it *(FIGURE 16B)*.

note: The working yarn is almost always carried across on the wrong side of the fabric, where it won't show.

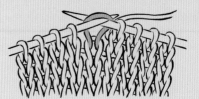

FIGURE 16A

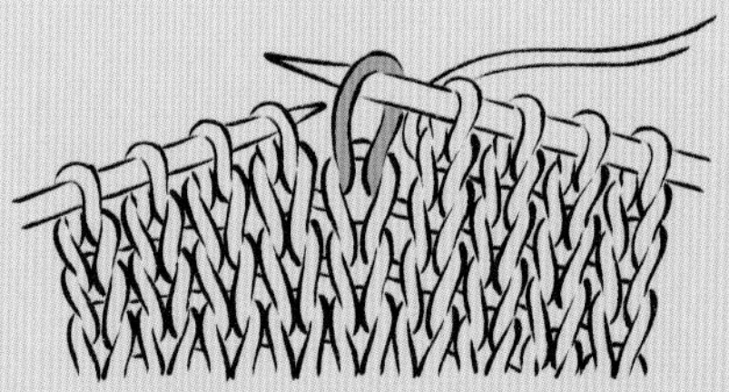

FIGURE 16B

crocheting slip stitch

This is a very simple edging that gives borders an even, finished look. It can also be used for joining two knit pieces.

1. Make a loop and hold it on your crochet hook.

2. With right side facing, place the hook through a knit stitch on the edge of your fabric.

3. Yarn over.

4. Pull yarn over through the loop on the hook.

5. Repeat steps 2 through 4 until you have worked your way around the area to be edged, stitch by stitch.

note: It is helpful to begin the edging where the yarn tails will be most easily hidden, such as at the center of the underarm.

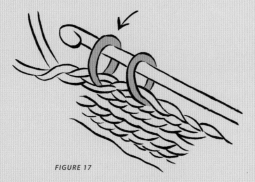

FIGURE 17

short rows

Short rows are all about shaping, and the name indicates exactly what you need to do to work them. You do not work an entire row from edge to edge as normal. Instead, turn your work around before reaching the edge of the knit piece and work your way back, stopping before you reach the other edge (the pattern will specify exactly where). Thus you can enlarge the cup part of a halter or sweater without actually making the edges bigger. If you do not want a hole when you turn the work, you should:

1. Bring your yarn forward to the purl position immediately before the turn, then slip the next stitch to your right needle as if to purl.

2. Turn work so the wrong side is facing you.

3. Bring yarn forward to purl position.

4. Return slipped stitch to right needle purlwise, then continue as directed.

resources

YARN SHOPS

There's nothing like being able to touch and see yarn. That's why it is important to find out where your local yarn shop is and pay a visit. Unfortunately, not everyone lives near a nice shop. The best place for yarn in your area may be a department store that carries only acrylic, while you want to work with wool. Don't despair. Thanks to the magic of the Internet, you can have a virtual yarn store in your very own home.

From ImaginKnits in San Francisco to Downtown Yarns in New York City (www.downtownyarns.com) to Halcyon Yarn in Bath, Maine (www.halcyonyarn. com), the United States is chock-full of knitting stores, and you are certain to find one that is right for you. You can find some of the yarns used in the projects in this book at www.yarn.com, www.theyarn exchange.com, and www.patternworks.com.

BOOKS

Big Book of Knitting by Katharina Buss (Sterling Publications, 2001)

Harmony Guides (Collins and Brown)

Kids Knitting by Melanie Falick (Artisan, 1998)

Knitted Embellishments by Nicky Epstein (Interweave Press, 1999)

Knitter's Almanac by Elizabeth Zimmermann (Schoolhouse Press, 1974)

The Knitter's Companion by Vicki Square (Interweave Press, 1996)

The Knitter's Handy Book of Patterns by Ann Budd (Interweave Press, 2002)

The Knitter's Handy Book of Sweater Patterns by Ann Budd (Interweave Press, 2004)

Knitting Around by Elizabeth Zimmermann (Schoolhouse Press, 1981)

The Knitting Experience: Book 1: The Knit Stitch and *Book 2: The Purl Stitch* by Sally Melville (XRX Books, 2002 and 2003)

Knitting from the Top by Barbara Walker (Schoolhouse Press, 1972)

Knitting without Tears by Elizabeth Zimmermann (Schoolhouse Press, 1971)

Needle Felting: Art Techniques and Projects by Anne Einset Vickrey with Patricia Spark and Linda Van Alstyne (Craft Works Publishing, 2002)

Socks Soar on Two Circular Needles by Cat Bordi (Passing Paws Press, 2001)

Stitch 'n Bitch: The Knitter's Handbook, Stitch 'n Bitch Nation, and *Stitch 'n Bitch: A Knitter's Design Journal* by Debbie Stoller (Workman Publishing, 2004, 2004, and 2005)

A Treasury of Knitting Patterns, A Second Treasury of Knitting Patterns, Charted Knitting Designs, and *A Fourth Treasury of Knitting Patterns* by Barbara Walker (Schoolhouse Press, 1981, 1998, 1998, and 2000)

Vogue Knitting: The Ultimate Knitting Book (Sixth & Spring Books, 2002)

MAGAZINES

Interweave Knits. Full of gorgeous patterns, *Interweave Knits* is a delight to look through. The magazine usually has something for everyone in its pages—from patterns for challenging, inventively constructed garments to simple gifty projects. In each issue, a knitting technique is thoughtfully explored in depth. Find it on the Web at www.interweave.com/knit.

Rebecca. You can find this German pattern magazine (which is loaded with exciting designs aimed at the younger set) in better yarn stores.

Rowan. This British pattern magazine not only has superb designs but also features techniques, fibers, and knitwear designs. Again, you will find it in yarn stores or on the Web at www.rowanyarns.co.uk.

Vogue Knitting. Packed with interesting, contemporary designs and the latest knitting news, this is the magazine you are most likely to find at your local yarn shop. It has also spawned a new magazine aimed at a younger, hipper crowd called *knit.1.* Find them on the Web at www.vogueknitting.com and www.knit1mag.com.

MISCELLANEOUS

Ask relatives or elderly friends if they have any knitting books or patterns you could borrow or have. A brief visit to the attic will sometimes yield a wealth of treasures.

Visit garage sales or thrift stores for patterns, books, and maybe even extra yarn and needles.

Visit the Internet for patterns and advice. One of my favorite sites is www.yesterknits.com, which boasts the largest collection of vintage knitting patterns in the world.

Search out vintage magazines, like *Ladies' Home Journal, Needlecraft, American Home,* and *McCall's Needlework.* You may be able to find these at garage sales, antique shops, and thrift stores, or in someone's attic.

SOCIAL OPPORTUNITIES

You don't have to knit alone if you don't want to! Here are some suggestions.

Take classes at your local yarn shop.

Join a knitting group. The Knitting Guild Association has many chapters. Find the one nearest you at www.tkga.com.

Start your own knitting group with a few friends.

Attend a Knit-Out, sponsored by the Craft Yarn Council. Knit-Outs take place in September and are forums for sharing finished projects, learning new stitches, and getting free patterns and advice. For more information on the next one near you, visit www.craftyarncouncil.com/knitoutbrochure.html.

Knit for charity. Visit www.tkga.com for information about Warm Up America and other organizations.

Knit in public. Knitters and nonknitters often will want to chat about their experiences and the project you're working on. It's a welcome touch of small-town living in an increasingly urban existence.

ONLINE RESOURCES

There are millions of links you could follow when you type *knitting* into a search engine. Here are a few of the better sites:

www.craftyarncouncil.com The Web site of the Craft Yarn Council of America (the yarn industry's trade association) raises awareness of all things yarn related by offering free patterns, advice, links to discussion groups, and information about how to join or start a knitting group.

www.knitting.about.com This site purports to be the most organized free pattern resource, and it truly has a wealth of patterns available to download. It also has a highly useful stitch pattern library.

www.knitty.com This stylish online magazine features great free patterns, interesting articles,

book and product reviews, and a coffee shop discussion forum. It is published four times a year and is very user friendly.

www.stitchnbitch.org This is the home of Stitch 'n Bitch Chicago, but don't assume this means they don't have your regional interests at heart. This site offers links to Stitch 'n Bitch groups all over the world. They also have a shop that features hip knit-themed T-shirts and totes.

www.tkga.com The Knitting Guild Association is a nonprofit organization of individuals and guilds. It has an official magazine, *Cast On*; a message board; and information about national and regional conferences. It's also a wonderful link to knit-for-charity sites.

You will also find a wealth of knit-centric blogs if you take a little time to browse around.

knitting abbreviations

ABBREVIATION	MEANING
alt	alternate
beg	beginning
bl	block
bo	bind off
cc	contrasting color
dble	double
dec	decrease
dp	double-pointed needle
foll	following
gm	gram
inc	increase
k	knit
lp(s)	loop(s)
mc	main color
oz	ounce
p	purl
patt	pattern
psso	pass slipped stitch over
rem	remaining
rep	repeat
rs	right side
rnd(s)	round(s)
sk	skip

ABBREVIATION	MEANING
sl	slip
sl st	slip stitch
ssk	slip, slip, knit
st(s)	stitch(es)
st st	stockinette stitch
tog	together
ws	wrong side
yo	yarn over

SYMBOL	MEANING
* *	repeat what is between the asterisks a specified number of times
( )	repeat what is between the parentheses as many times as specified

SOME HELPFUL TERMS

YARN DOUBLE	use 2 strands of yarn simultaneously, held together as if they are a single strand
YARN TRIPLE	use 3 strands of yarn simultaneously, held together as if they are a single strand
WORK EVEN	continue in the same stitch pattern, with no increases or decreases, until futher directed

index